FROM THISTLE TO FERN

Text and photography by

EILIDH MACPHERSON

farmingscotland.com

Photographs

Front Cover and Inside Front: Musterer, Cameron Scott on Nokomai Station
Landscape: The Hakateramea Valley
Half Title Page: Church of the Good Shepherd, Lake Tekapo
Title Page: Farmed deer, Glendhu Road, Waimumu
Below: Shepherd, horse and dogs, Kyeburn Station
Acknowledgements page: Romneys at saleyards, Omarau
Opposite Contents: Moving a mob of Aberdeen Angus Cattle, Mount Linton Station
Contents: 11000 Sheep on the run, Mount Linton Station
Opposite Introduction: Glenorchy
Opposite Preface: Pat McNamee, Mt Nicholas Station muster
Preface Page: Blade Shears, Author competing at Mossburn Shears,
Ready for shearing Dunstan Peaks Station
Following Preface: Road to Nowhere – Up the Hakateramea Valley

Copyright details

From Thistle to Fern
First published in Great Britain by farmingscotland.com in 2005,
Shepherds Cottage, Eynort, Isle of Skye

First Edition

ISBN 0-9502579-2-3 / 978-0-9502579-2-1

Printed by Highland Printers Limited
Henderson Road, Inverness IV1 1SP

My High Country Man
my Dad pictured on our hill at home
on the shores of Loch Brittle, Isle of Skye

To my Dad and Mum – William and Una MacPherson

Gu athair agus mo mhathair – Uilleam agus Una Mac a'Phearsain

Moran tháing airson a h-uile rud a rinn thu.

Se aite boidheach ann a tuathanach ard anns New Zealand
Ach bithidh mo chride gu direach mo latha anns na Gaeltachd anns Alba

ACKNOWLEDGEMENTS

There are so many people to mention who have helped me out over the past few years while this book was but a dream - at the drawing board stage. Anna Van der Schuit and her family entertained me over Christmas and the Millenium, while I worked out what I wanted to do. Special thanks to Wendy Patterson and her family at Dunstan Peaks, then Una and Dean Drysdale and also Viv Oag who let me use their houses as a base for a couple of months apiece. Thanks to Bruce and Jude Hamilton, Winton, who have been like parents to me on all my New Zealand trips and constantly e-mail me to see where I am and how I'm doing. Maree Clarke of Pahiatua's door was always open on my way past and thanks to Donna Hamilton and Mike Lunn for the house sitting stint at Mount Linton. I would also like to thank Trevor and Janice Middleton who gave me a start shearing in Southland on my first three trips out and have always been very hospitable. I am also indebted to Sarah Dowie, my lawyer mate, her parents and Mark Billcliff, Trevor Copeland, Ross Hasslemore, Ronnie, Jo and Zac Moore, Andrew Dagg, Priscilla Stevens, Annie Wallace, Keri Williams, Iain and Kathryn Davidson, Carolyn McLaren, Andrew and Nicola Hamilton, John Hamilton, cousin Neil & Steph MacPherson and family: David, Michael and Rebecca, Jacqui,

Wayne and Ben Ingram, Morag McDonald 0(ex-Skye) now Taupo and Darryl.

On the work front, I must thank Hugh Stringleman of the New Zealand Farmer, John Hart of the Shearing Magazine, Steven Mason of the Southland Times and Vicki Lunn and Diane Bishop of the Otago Southland Farmer for printing my articles and keeping me afloat. A big thank you to Jennifer Sharpe of the National Bank for having faith in me.

Without the cooperation and kindness of so many owners and employees on the stations, this book would have been impossible.

SOUTH ISLAND

Mount Linton: Dave and Diane Walsh, Paul McCarthy, Bart Sherbourne, Johnny Goodwin, Ronald Watt, Robert Grant, Mike Lunn, Glenn Prebble, Andrew Chrystal and Jo the Cook. Jim Malcolm, Western Southland Shearing and employees (too many to mention)
Glenaray: David Pickney
Galloway: Andrew Preston
Kyeburn: Nicolas, and Hamish Mackenzie
Ben Ohau: Simon and Priscilla Cameron
Braemar: Hamish McKenzie
Ben Omar: 'Ginger' & John Anderson, Lindsay Purvis and Rick Aubrey

Glenmore: John and Anne Murray
Nokomai: Brian, Ann, Frank and James Hore, Daniel Price, Cameron Scott, Chris Anderson, Matt Black, Mark, 'Stretch' aka Danny Hayes, Jason Woodhouse and Kit Fox
Walter Peak: John and Sharon Templeton, Hamish McKnight, Hamish Mcdonald, Grant McMaster, Cameron Scott and Mark Stalker
Mount Nicholas: Robert, Linda, Kate and David Butson, Pat McNamee and Matt Menlove.

NORTH ISLAND

Pipi Bank: Bill and Ngaire Speedy
Araparwanui: Mr & Mrs Brian MacKinnon
Waipu: Ross Finlayson

Last but by no means least my family and friends at home in Scotland who helped me and kept me going with letters, e-mails and the odd phone call during my two and a half year stint in New Zealand. Namely: Mum & Dad, Lindsay, Allan and Caitriana, Fiona McArthur, Ali Gordon, Fionna and Dick Haigh, Beth Bidwell and Mike Rivington, Iain McGillivary and Jacqui Pattison, Heather and Chris Dibble, Catherine Ann Dick, Maggie Macdonald, Mags Harvey, Jock Gibson, John Kidd and Jim & Linda Orr.

CONTENTS

INTRODUCTION

The Scots and the New Zealanders have ties dating back to the 1840's and well before. It must be noted that the first person of Scottish descent to arrive in New Zealand in 1772 was James Cook – this point is often overlooked as he was brought up in Yorkshire, but his father came from Roxburgh in the Scottish Borders, where he had been a farm labourer.

There are many factors contributing to the Scots emigrating to America, Canada, Australia and New Zealand. As the Lowland and English Landlords moved the people of the Highlands and Islands off the land, to be replaced by more profitable Cheviot sheep, conditions in Scottish industrial cities became crowded and as the old customs of clan, covenant and communities seemed to be disappearing, emigration and the opportunity of owning some land was a bright option.

> Where are those bold pilots now?
> Alas! They're buried in the ground,
> Their children scattered the world around,
> Their houses levelled to a mound
>> To make room for farmers' sheep
>> And lowland cattle fat and sleek,
>> Grazing in the very street
>> Where once Holm village stood.
>>> John MacKinnon
>>> Napier, New Zealand, 1898

But it was religious, Scottish immigrants who had a major influence on early developments in the South Island . The first ship – The Bengal Merchant – sailed from Port Glasgow on 25 October 1839 arriving in Dunedin (Gaelic for Edinburgh –'Duneidean') on the 20 February 1840 – just two weeks after the signing of the treaty of Waitangai – with 122 passengers aboard accompanied by the minister –John Macfarlane.

These Scots had been members of the Church of Scotland and had broken away to form a Free Church; being able to choose their own ministers rather than the state or local landlords appointing them.

It is estimated that by the early 1870's one in three New Zealanders of the then 220 000 population were Scottish Presbyterians. And even today the majority of Kiwis can boast some Scottish connection in their lineage.

The early settlers endured hardships, taking weeks if not months to drove stock to their runs, through dense tussock, wild Irishman scrub and spear grass as well as fording bridgeless rivers and boggy ground.

Initially some of the runholders in the High Country were English (Sassenachs) but, due to the extremes of climate (Sahara type summers to Baltic winters), high winds and isolation in the Mackenzie Country, the Poms moved to warmer, more populated climes and left the MacKenzie Country to the Scottish shepherds. These hardy souls, brought up in windswept glens and heather clad slopes of the Scottish Highlands, were well accustomed to severe weather conditions and their canine cohorts – the collie dogs were used to operating on similar terrain and working at a distance from their masters. Around 80% of the inhabitants were Scottish with the majority being Gaelic speaking.

To this day the area still has a Highland air with the skirl of the pipes, kilts worn at functions, highland gatherings and the names: Burnett, Cameron, MacKenzie, Murray and Urquhart are still household entities on MacKenzie stations.

Sheep were predominantly reared on these runs and the main income generated was from the sale of their wool. Once the properties were fully stocked, only a limited local market was available for the sale of mutton. Carcases were boiled down for tallow, as there was no alternative.

By 1882, two Scots, William Davidson and Thomas Brydone were instrumental in changing the whole structure of sheep farming in New Zealand by making the first shipment of refrigerated lamb (frozen) to the UK and opening up expansive overseas markets. This factor revolutionised New Zealand farming: station country remained as wool growing areas, but the lower hills produced lambs to be finished on the fertile plains.

Thomas Brydone was to the fore once again pioneering methods in topdressing, using lime to restore deteriorating grassland and increase stock numbers on the lower ground.

> 'S gur h-e Otago am fearann priseil,
> Le cruithneachd finealt 'se cinntinn ann,
> Coirce 's grainnseach gu torach, lanmhor,
> Is por gun aireamh a'fas air t'fhonn.

> It's in Otago the land is fertile,
> And wheat that is finest is growing there,
> Oats with grain that is filled with kernels,
> And plants unnumbered the soil supports.

From these hard pioneering days, New Zealand has become one of the leading agricultural nations in the world in terms of production, exporting and technology.

Since these early days, some stations are no longer, some have been sub-divided for soldier settlement and others have changed hands many times. In general the low ground has become more productive with top-dressing and break cropping and the higher country is very much farmed in the same way as it was, used as summer grazing. Beef cattle, deer and tourism are other enterprises common place on many stations nowadays.

The Scottish settlers have left an impression that few others have matched: an inheritance that cannot be measured in monetary terms alone and they have influenced the social strata, the attitudes and the morality of this island nation.

PREFACE

The clock struck twelve – lunchtime. 'Thank goodness', I thought as I pushed the last lamb down the porthole and pulled the stop cord. With every muscle aching, I eased myself down off the raised board and made my way to the sink to wash down my arms, which were smeared with grease and green filth from fingertips to armpits.

With borrowed shearing gear, moccasins at least two sizes too big, shearing pants quite the reverse and the fact that I hadn't lifted a handpiece for at least six months, the morning had lasted an eternity. My slimline Fagans (shearing pants) were under severe pressure. The live weight gained from ad lib feeding over the festive period would have been a joy to any finishing farmer, but to me it felt as if my stomach was being operated on every time I bent over to crutch another lamb.

As we wandered out of the dimly lit shed into glorious sunshine, I was beginning to wonder if I had lost the plot. .... a new millennium and here I was back on the board, suffering big time on my first day, head down, bum up. Surely I could do something else and see more of the awesome countryside and sunshine in New Zealand, rather than just the inside of the shearing sheds and making do with sight seeing on wet days.

I had been captivated by the high country and read numerous books on the stations during my previous three shearing trips to New Zealand. Realising that the Scottish angle had not been covered, I decided to follow in the footsteps of my kinsmen who had pioneered vast tracts of this amazing country, taking up runs, developing them and introducing sheep, some hundred and fifty years before. Many of their descendants are still farming them today and the Scottish hills and glens are remembered in countless station, creek and mountain range names across the country.

I enjoyed every minute of my travels round the Sheep Stations of NZ, was welcomed with open arms and received true High Country hospitality in every sense of the word.

South Island Stations

- Glenmore
- Ben Ohau
- Ben Omar

Mount Nicholas •
Walter Peak •

• Kyeburn

• Galloway

• Nokomai

• Glenaray

Mount Linton •

Andrew 'Shepherd' Crystall, and canine cohorts, move sheep into the Mount Linton yards for drenching

MOUNT LINTON STATION

My dream of visiting the high country stations had finally become reality – I set out from the country town of Winton, where I had been staying on farm with friends, with mixed emotions of excitement and trepidation. Destination: – Mount Linton.

Several years earlier, on my last trip to the 'Land of the Big White Cloud,' I had visited Mount Linton Station with my brother Allan and his friend Angus Davidson, aka 'Goose.' Sheep dipping/spraying 30 000 ewes was in full swing and we three Scottish Highlanders were in absolute awe of the whole scale of the operation. One of the shepherds had taken us out to a hill block to muster a mob of 11 000 ewes. At home sheep are grazed with roughly six acres to the sheep, not six sheep to the acre and a farm with 2000 or 3000 ewes is considered large.

Passing through the dingy coalmining town of Ohai, the stark contrast and beauty of the rolling green hills of Mount Linton unfolded beyond.

As I turned the last corner towards the station buildings, the colossal woolshed and covered yards loomed into the horizon. Several shepherds were busily occupied drafting ewes.

My tour guide for the morning, Assistant Farm Manager Dave Walsh, pulled up on cue in a white Toyota Hilux laden with an assortment of dogs. Realising that I was Scottish, Dave excitedly announced, "our cattle manager is from Aberdeenshire – you might understand him."

As we drove round the 130km of station roads he filled me in on the history and farming practices of Mount Linton which is situated on the eastern side of the Takitimu Mountains and lies 56kms north west of the most Southerly City in New Zealand – Invercargill. Covering some 13 000ha in area, this rolling to steep property, which lies at an altitude of 120 to 800m, is small in comparison to some of the high country stations in Central Otago, further north.

"The property was established in 1854, but the records of ownership until 1903 are vague as it changed hands frequently. W.J.A. McGregor, grandfather of Alastair McGregor, the current Executive Chairman purchased it at this juncture, for its grazing ability of the hill country," said Dave.

J W Raymond is the first person recorded to hold Run 156, the now Mt Linton. His tenure was to run for 14 years from August 7 1857 but he transferred it to William Cameron (whose brother Donald had Nokomai Station). Other names to be associated with the station before the McGregors took over in 1903 are: John Slade Manning, Thomas Morrel Macdonald and William Russell, Alexander McIntosh Clark, the Bank of New South Wales and a Reginald Mackinnon.

William James Annan McGregor, a Presbyterian minister's son was born at Kaiapoi in 1874. He was educated at Amberley before he started farming at Kaikoura, where he married Ellen Boyd in 1900. He took Mount Linton Station up in partnership with Edward Gates in 1903, before he went out on his own.

WJA McGregor was very much a committee man, being involved with the local mine, railway, County council, A&P Show, NZ Meat Producers Board, Invercargill Rotary Club as well as serving as an elder in the Nightcaps Presbyterian church.

Apparently previous owners suffered from isolation, rabbit infestation and heavy flood and snow losses, but Mr McGregor turned the tables by large scale reseeding. His son Noel followed suit, importing machinery from England and clearing around 500ha per year and increasing production.

As a young boy Noel McGregor was friendly with Douglas Pick of neighbouring Birchwood Station. Mr Pick, of English descent noted, as a ten year old boy, that:

We had not long been in Birchwood before realizing that we were the only English people there. All the rest were Scots from the Isles or West of Scotland.

Some had been crofters – such good neighbours they proved to be too. Most were new arrivals and I remember them coming and how they lived and worked. They took up blocks of land – 500 to 800 acres and they dug into the hillside and made a hole of 15-20 feet back, 10 –12 ft wide and roofed it with timbers over which they laid manuka brush and put a mound of clay on top. The front they timbered up and the door was a split chaff sack, the table a packing case, the chair a box and the bunk a pole frame with a bag mattress. The fireplace was in the back end clay wall with a sod chimney. They got their water from the stream.

Their first job was to clear the land and get in a crop of oats and neaps before sowing down to grass. These men roughed it – and they all made good. They, that is, the married men, left their wives and bairns in Dunedin or Invercargill until the first house was built. They were lonely and rarely met other men. Dad had four children, so he called a meeting in the station woolshed to discuss a Settlers' Association and plan a school, a meeting place and a church. It transpired that there was no money for such buildings and it was decided that meetings and church continue to use the woolshed, except when it was needed at shearing time. School was a problem as the woolshed was too large and draughty in winter.

There were nine children of school age but the Southland Education Board could not build a school for so few children. The lack of a school was solved by the cheese factory manager who offered one of the front rooms of his house.

Church was a monthly occasion. We all went to the woolshed. People came in all sorts of vehicles. The parson was a Presbyterian of course. He hammered the pulpit (wool table) and I was sure he was only preaching to me. Hellfire and brimstone pits and lakes of fire. How did he know so much about me? All my wicked past paraded before me in a flash. Lies I had told, orchards I had robbed, and windows I had smashed. The time I had tried to smoke Dad's pipe in the dunny. Girls pigtails I had pulled or tied to the inkwell holes in my desk. That stack I had tried to burn and that recent escapade at church when Noel McGregor and I put old McKay's buggy shafts through the fence and yoked up his horse so that the buggy was on one side and the horse on the other! Wasn't there a stink about that? Nobody knew, or so I thought – but that parson seemed to know.

What good people these Scots were. Every time they called they brought a dozen eggs or a plate of scones and always enquired about the 'coos' and the bairns and the wee wife, in that order. If a Scottish woman heard of anybody sick, they would arrange for one of their strapping girls to come and take over and do the housework and look after the children. How careful those folk were with the pennies but how generous they were in good causes.

James Noel McGregor, the second son, was educated at John McGlashan College, before he took on part of the management of Mount Linton following the death of his older brother Hector in 1925. Noel married Leslie Holbeche on 8 January 1938 and they had two children: Alastair and Virginia.

Over a thirty seven year period Noel had more than doubled the stock carrying capacity of the property: from 11 000 sheep, 4 500 lambs and 120 cattle in 1925 to 25 000 sheep, 18 000 lambs, 3000 cattle and 1200 calves by 1957. Nowadays stock numbers tally at an amazing 60 000 ewes, 16 000 ewe hoggets and 6000 other sheep, 1700 breeding cattle and 1550 followers.

Noel was instrumental in the developing of private hill country in New Zealand, being the first landowner to employ a pilot to fly on a 100-tonne load of superphosphate in 1949.

He was tragically killed by gunshot on 5 May 1958 which the Southland Times reported: 'Southland has lost one of the most remarkable farmers in its history.' His son Alastair took over the management of Mount Linton.

Prior to the First World War, Mount Linton covered some 61 000 acres. With the Government intervening for soldier settlement, it was consequently reduced to 15 500ha. Alastair retired 2500ha for conservation purposes in lieu of a tenure review, which involved granting a freehold title to the rest of the property, bringing the spread to its present size.

Mount Linton property now boasts 4500ha of developed grassland, 3500ha of over sown tussock country, 240ha of radiata pine trees, 250ha of fenced off native bush reserve and the remainder is native tussock. Paddocks on the hill country are around 150ha in size and on the cultivated ground are on average 50ha. They are mob-stocked and grazed in rotation. Over 130km of road, ribbons round the station and an estimated 800km of fencing covers the contours and plains of paddocks and easy-move stock lanes. Natural Woloncough gravel, which is found on the property is used as road metal, so is a great saving.

The Station, one of New Zealand's largest, privately owned, pastoral agribusinesses is run as a company and incorporates several other farms further afield which are used for stud and finishing purposes. It is also stratified as such with managers on each outlying property, a cattle manager, stock manager and assistant manager (Dave) on site, with General Manager, Paul

McCarthy overseeing the whole operation. Major shareholder, Alastair McGregor has the final say.

The company's objective is to be pre-eminent in the production of livestock and in achieving long-term financial returns for its' shareholders. Other employees include: 2 office staff, 10 shepherds, 1 tractor driver, 1 dozer operator, 1 truck driver, 3 domestic/garden staff, and a cook. Two properties of 480ha have recently been leased at Ashburton, on the Canterbury Plains.

After a thorough tour and run down on the history, policies and production of the station,

Dave dropped me off at the cattle yards where cattle manager Ronald Watt (Scottie) and shepherd Michael Lunn (Polly) were drafting out cull cows.

"You'll be coming to the speed shear in the local pub tonight, we're supplying the sheep," Dave said as I was climbing out of the truck.

"Yes, I'm actually covering it for the Southland Times," I replied.

"Well stop in for a shower and your dinner beforehand at the house," he said before taking off towards the homestead. This was my

introduction to High Country kindness, not unlike the Highland hospitality encountered by those who have travelled to the Highlands and Islands of Scotland.

I spent the rest of the afternoon helping Ronald and Mike coax cattle up the race in between periodically clicking away on my camera to get the perfect shot.

Mount Linton Station, claimed to be the most productive station property per acre in New Zealand, has employed the 'Real McCoy' to oversee their expanding Aberdeen Angus Stud

Out the back of Mount Linton Station. There are 6000 sheep in the paddock in the foreground.

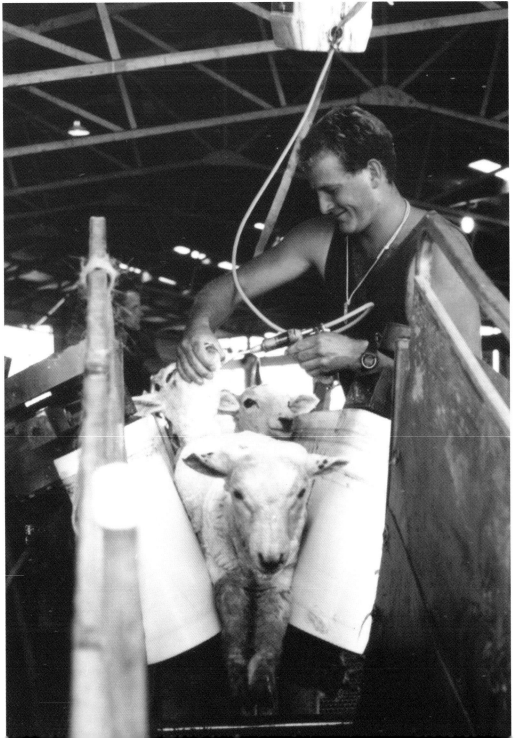

and commercial cattle enterprises. Born under the 'Northern Lights' at Dufftown, some thirty miles North West of the City of Aberdeen, Scotland, Ronald (31), alias 'Scottie,' has certainly landed on his feet in Southland, holding the position of Cattle Manager on this prominent station.

"Farming is very similar out here to back home, but done on a much bigger scale, more intensively," Scottie commented.

Hereford cattle used to roam the green hills of Mount Linton, but when neighbouring Wilanda Downs Station sold up, Alastair McGregor bought some Aberdeen Angus stud cows, which originated from the Canterbury, Te Mania Stud. Since then Mount Linton have gone into an AI program and imported semen from America and Australia.

Over the past five years the Angus Stud numbers have risen annually from 280 cows in 1996. Last year there were 540, this year 600 calved and 800 including the heifers are in-calf for next season.

Every year 400 to 600 cows are artificially inseminated with Angus semen from proven sires – using CIDR's to synchronize ovulation. Selected Angus bulls are used on the remainder and on the commercial herd with three or four running with each mob. There are also eight or nine mobs, which are single sire mated – these bulls cover 40 to 45 dams each.

Record keeping of the stud cattle plays a large part of the cattle manager's role with all the pure Angus calves are weighed, ear tagged and recorded at birth. The Herefords have been crossed with Angus, of which 120 are kept each year as replacements for the commercial herd. These beasts are injected with 2ml of Prostaglandin, to bring on heat in 48 hours and are then covered by ten bulls – this method condenses calving into a six-week period. There are only forty pure Herefords left now.

The cattle play a vital role in utilizing the grassland thus improving the grazing for the sheep," explained Dave. "During the winter

Robert Grant drenches sheep on the conveyor belt.

months the cattle are hot wired on the tops of the back blocks and run in one mob of 1200, with the heifers separately."

Before wintering the cattle are treated with a pour-on for lice and injected with Selenium and Copper. The latter seems to be very deficient on the Station.

Two hundred bulls (150 1yo and 50 2yo), which are sold privately from the station each year, have dramatically increased the gross margin of the cattle enterprise on Mount Linton. The sires are selected for home use by breeding values, birth weights and live weight gain and the remainder are sorted into price lines to show

prospective buyers around. The average weight of the bulls at weaning is 260kgs. Assistant farm manager, David Walsh enthuses, "Over the past few years the cattle live weights have increased by 45kgs – this is due to increased genetics and improved cattle management."

At weaning, heifer calves (for replacements) are placed in three pits in lots of two hundred for six months. These consist of a self-feed silage pit with push up barriers and wood chipped surfaced lying areas. The steers and cull heifer calves go to the finishing farms, with five hundred being sold at 450kgs to 'Five Star' feedlot at Ashburton – making Mount Linton the largest single supplier

to Five Star. This enterprise, New Zealand's only feedlot, carries 12 000 head of cattle at any time and supplies the Asian market, finishing the beasts to 750kgs.

Every beast, including calves are TB tested annually by the Ministry of Agriculture. A number of years ago Mount Linton had a reactor, which was presumably transmitted by wild pigs from the scrub on the property. It has now been clear for a year – C1 status and all offspring are finished. Purchasing cattle from a C1 status property immediately transfers the vendors status to the new owner.

That evening, following a refreshing shower

Moving a mob of 200 Aberdeen Angus cattle with Scottie and Robert, out the back of the Station.

and meal, courtesy of Dave's wife Diane, I headed back to Ohai and the pink coloured pub – 'The Pick and Shears'.

As I walked from my wee Honda Civic towards the pub, I met Mick Keay from Whangarei, a shearer who had competed at my annual shearing competition on the Isle of Skye the previous year. He was shearing for a local contractor for a few months before heading north.

The pub was beginning to fill up with budding gun shearers all gearing for a fast time and a share of the spoils. Juniors, locals, seniors, veterans and open candidates raced against the clock to secure some of the limelight and a place in the four-man final. Each competitor had to shear one lamb as quickly as possible, but still maintaining a quality job. Three judges eyed the

finished product and gave a green light for 'go' and a red one for 'no'. At least two green lights were required to make the final. Over the past few years Speed Shears have become part of the New Zealand culture not only in country pubs but also in town garden bars and nightclubs.

Veterans entertained the crowd in the almost tropical conditions in the packed Ohai Hotel. Local man Ken Jackson fended off his brother Dave to take first place by just over 6 seconds and local contractor Jim Malcolm of Western Southland Shearing, who organises Mount Linton's machine shearing was third, only 0.06secs slower.

As a shearer I was itching to have a go, but refrained from making a spectacle of myself as I hadn't lifted a handpiece for at least 6 months

and not shorn a lamb since my last visit to New Zealand in 1994.

Darren Murray, a ganger for Jim Malcolm, lifted the trophy for the best local with a speedy time of 40.68secs. Successful open circuit competitor and NZ Team member for the 2000 World Shearing Championships in Bloemfontein, South Africa, Darrin Forde was beaten by a blow – 0.14sec – by Cartwright Terry of Cambridge, in the North Island.

Most of the people whom I'd met on the Station earlier in the day were there for the evening entertainment with a few extras to whom I was introduced. Stock Manager, Bart Sherbourne suggested that I should meet up with them all and report on the Mossburn Hack Races in a couple of weeks time.

Darrin Forde whips out a lamb in no time at the Speed Shears in Ohai.

Darren Murray with his shearing spoils.

Hundreds of sheep await a drench in the massive yards.

GLENARAY STATION

Lying directly opposite Argyle Station in the Waikaia Valley is Glenaray – the largest, privately owned, pastoral property in Southland. It started off as Run No 328 in February 1860 and had five Scottish owners before being purchased by the Pinckney family in 1898.

Scotsman, David Hood was granted the licence for 14 years for this run, which is estimated to have been 36 000 acres. The boundaries, as with neighbouring Runs 326 and 327, remained "to be fixed", ran up to the top of the Umbrella Mountains near the now township of Waikaia.

Born in Haddington, East Lothian in 1818, to William (a shipmaster) and Ann (nee Simpson) Hood, David emigrated to New Zealand in 1852. Little information could be found on him, other than he died at Halfway Bush, Roslyn aged 76.

David Hood sold Run No. 328 to John Gow of Invermay, East Taieri in 1861. John Gow (aged 51, born at Caputh, Perthshire, 1801), had also arrived in New Zealand in 1852, but initially took up land on what is now the town of Mosgiel on the outskirts of Dunedin.

He travelled out from Scotland with his sister Isabella, brother John and his wife Catherine on the Agra, which docked at Port Chalmers on 4 May 1852. The Gow family had previously been tenants of the Duke of Atholl, farming 'Fungarth' near Dunkeld, Perthshire. Gow comes from the Gaelic 'gobha', meaning blacksmith and is a sect of the clan MacPherson.

In John Gow's time the station was referred to as Gows' Run. He had stocked the run with cattle and topped the Dunedin markets for several years. On his death in August 1873, the property was handed over to trustees, who sold out the following year to David McKellar of Waimea Plains, who also purchased neighbouring Waikaia Downs – Run no.424, some 19 000 acres from Francis Fielding.

David McKellar who was born at Achahoish, Argyllshire on 28 July 1829 grew up on Lockhead, on the Duke of Argyll's land, where his father was tacksman. David trained as a surveyor and civil engineer before travelling to Australia, where a cousin – Dugald Macpherson had a sheep property in Victoria. It was 1855

before he moved to New Zealand to join his brother Peter. Initially they owned Longridge and Waimea runs in Southland. The purchase of Waikaia Plains in August 1867 followed the sale of Waimea earlier in the year to G.M. Bell of Tasmania for £65,000.

David's surveying background was an added bonus during his explorations of the Wakatipu area in 1857. He is considered to be the first European man to see the North arm of Lake Wakatipu when he was exploring the Von and Oreti rivers. McKellar Flat, which is now on Mount Nicholas Station, still bears his name.

David McKellar relinquished the run (both Glenaray and Wakaia) to his cousin John McKellar after only 13 months of ownership. He then lived outside Invercargill for ten years, before buying Brooksdale, Tapanui from his brother John in 1887. Following a trip to Mexico in 1880, David sold Brooksdale in 1882 and moved with his wife Jane Catherine (nee Skene) to pastures new – 300 000 acres in New Mexico. His wire fences apparently did not go down well with the neighbouring Mexican farmers and

David was assassinated on 29 July 1892.

It is assumed that it was John McKellar who changed the name of the station to Glenaray. He was also of Argyllshire origin, fifth son from a family of seven boys and two girls, born at Kilmorich on 6 June 1839. His father Donald was Tacksman of Stronchullin, on the shores of Loch Fyne, South Knapdale, Argyll. The township of Inveraray lies at the head of Loch Fyne with Glen Aray nearby.

He too had been a surveyor and arrived in Dunedin in 1859 where he was employed by the Survey Department of the Otago Provincial Council. After a couple of months working around Dunedin, he was taken into the office of the head surveyor, JT Thomson, and shown a map of the Otago province, with huge blank spaces of uncharted back country – some 8000 square miles of it. The Land Office wanted McKellar to survey it as quickly as possible as pioneers were submitting claims from every corner and the authorities had unreliable mapping on which to register each new run.

Setting out on 11 Dec 1861, with two others to help him: John Goldie and James Bryce, he mapped Hawea and Wanaka areas then Te Anau and Manapouri districts, Lakes Hauroko and Monowai and the Takatimiu Mountains. On 3rd June 1863 they viewed the Sounds on the West Coast for the first time and named what they saw, Caswell Sound. James also named the mountain on which they stood Mt Pisgan after where Moses had viewed the Promised Land. The trio encountered many dangers and I'm sure they would have had a tale or two to tell!

John McKellar ran Glenaray (now including Runs 424 and 436A) until 1883 when he was declared bankrupt. The disastrous winter of 1878, followed by an infestation of rabbits ruined him and from this point on, the station was taken over by the Bank of Australasia. Run 436A – the 'Lakes' – which covered some 25 000 acres was leased by John McKellar. It was also passed on to the Bank and has remained a part of Glenaray ever since.

There was one more Scottish run holder at Glenaray – this time in the shape of – John Walker in 1890. It was claimed that he was a son of Johnny Walker of the red and blue label whisky fame, but it was more than likely an old wives' tale.

By 1895, Glenaray had changed hands once again – to Frank D. Morrah, who in turn sold out some three years later to George Pinckney in partnership with his two brother-in-laws, the Tripps. George Pinckney had married Edith Howard Tripp, whose brothers; Bernard Edward Tripp farmed at Woodbury, Geraldine and John Mowbary Tripp at Richmond, Tekapo.

Part of Moa Flat, which had originally covered 63 000 acres was also included in the sale of Waikaia Plains in 1904 and was then bought by Edith Howard Pinckney in 1905. This 34, 500-acre block was Run 436.

Another 662 acres were acquired in 1907 – Run 326A – from Finlay Stanislaus Murchison (born 1834), an exile of Ardnarf, Lochalsh, Ross-shire. He married a daughter of Angus McDonnell of Glengarry and came out to New Zealand with a family of eight. Three of the sons: Alex, Angus and John were renowned for their gold mining and illicit whisky distillation.

George Pinckney hailed from Millford Hill, Salisbury where his father was manager of Pinckney's Bank, which eventually became Lloyds. He was sent to Exeter College, Oxford to further his education but did not enjoy the academic side of things, preferring rowing at which he excelled. It was there he met Howard Tripp from Orari Gorge, South Canterbury and following a short spell working in his father's bank – he emigrated to New Zealand to fulfil his ambition to become a sheep farmer.

Orari Gorge Station was the first position for this 'green' young Englishman as a farm cadet. Soon after his arrival he was sent out to a backcountry hut with the head shepherd,

Murdoch MacLeod, for two weeks, to learn the finer points of shepherding. Further down the track, George said, "I learnt more about sheep in those two weeks than I was ever to learn from any other man."

George moved on from Orari to gain experience on other properties and to see a bit of the country. Riverslea, owned by J Brown and Murdoch McKay was one property on which he worked. Apparently McKay came from the Highlands of Scotland and was renowned for his good stockmanship and agricultural knowledge. He was always well presented in tailored Harris tweeds, with a shirt and tie and carried a 'cromag' (shepherds crook). His dog Glen at his heel, received all his commands in his native Gaelic tongue.

When George Pinckney took over Glenaray, he turned to Murdoch McKay as manager, as he had realised he had so much to learn about the running of such a huge operation. Murdoch held the fort while George took his new bride and two young children home to England. On their

return, McKay moved on to manage Hyde Home Station just five miles away and then in 1903 he purchased the homestead block of Hyde Home. He remained a close friend and advisor for George and came to be "boss of the shearing board" every shearing season. Murdoch McKay discussed and advised the best breed of sheep to run on the property.

Although the production of wool is of paramount importance to the run holder, other factors have also to be taken into consideration when deciding upon the type of sheep from which it is intended to breed; it is sometimes necessary to make alterations in policy. The aim at Glenaray has been to breed a sheep that will suit the type of country, that will produce a fleece as fine as possible, and yet, having both these characteristics, will be attractive to the farmer on the lower country who will eventually buy the cast ewes.

When the run was first acquired sheep were of a rather mixed breed and were found unsuitable for the proposed system of management. To standardise the type of sheep Mr G Pinckney introduced Merino rams, which were used until 1908, when Romneys were brought in and were used for 10 years. From 1918 to 1933 both Corriedales and Romneys were used, 60 Corriedale and 30 Romney rams being purchased each year during this period. From 1933 Romney rams only have been used. At present the Romney influence is strong, but the type of sheep being bred is fulfilling the three points mentioned previously: an active sheep, producing a fine but heavy fleece and attractive to the sheep and dairy farmer as a cast ewe.

To attain this almost dual type has not been by any means easy, particularly because sheep must be of a sound constitution and be agile to make full use of the high country.

NZ Journal of Ag. 1950

All shearing at Glenaray was done with blades until the Second World War broke out, forcing run holders to shear by machine, as there was such a shortage of blade shearers. There were no significant increases in sheep losses following the move to machine shearing.

Some of the risk and damage and loss from snow may be gained from the records of Glenaray, where in 1945 there was a loss of 3 700 sheep owing to heavy snow in April. In 1939, although heavy snow was recorded, losses were comparatively light, as the sheep were all in winter country.

One of the worst years was 1933 snow fell in April and snow raking had to be done from 20 April until 1 June. Between April and June 2000 ewes, 3000 lambs and 1000 wethers were lost. In 1918 and 1923 there were also heavy snow and losses of sheep, although neither year was as bad as 1933. Snow is one of the extremely unpleasant phases of life on a high-country run, and besides being a source of heavy financial loss, snow can, in a relatively short period of time, nullify the

work of many years.

NZ Journal of Ag. 1950

George Pinckney started to buy up neighbouring lowland farms to provide winter feed, utilise the high country and increase stock numbers. He began liming the Glenaray pastures to improve fertility in 1906. George had seen the wonderful results that Erskine Bowmar (yet another Scot) had achieved liming his Waimumu property, near Gore.

Prior to 1918, when the station was fenced, numerous boundary keepers were employed over the years to keep watch over the sheep. Archie McDonnell, Ralph Thomson and Julian Jackson, were a few, who spent months on end in the high country. The latter alias Jack Mac, because of the cape he wore, has become a legend and one of the huts still bears his name to this day.

George and Edith Pinckney had 'eight daughters and three sons' – the title of a book on Glenaray by Barbara Harper. The eldest son, Jack, was killed in action in 1918. It was Kathleen, the fourth daughter, who married Bill Pinckney, one of George's nephews, who came out from England as a cadet in 1922, who took over the running of Glenaray in 1948 when George died. Bill had served four years with the Argyll and Sutherland Highlanders, two years in France and two in Ireland.

By 1950 a new company, made up of: Bill and Kathleen Pinckney, her brothers Harold and Bindy and her sons Peter and George, was formed to manage the station, the first time since 1898. W (Bill) Pinckney Ltd, who had first purchased shares in 1925, bought the station for £100,000.

Bill went on with developing the property, fencing and subdividing paddocks, increasing the holding capacity of the station all the while as well as improving stock quality and wool weights. He handed over the running of the station to his two sons, Peter and George before he passed away in 1973.

Peter married Ann Lowry and raised their three children: David, Thomas and Anna at Glenaray. Unfortunately Peter and Ann were tragically killed in a helicopter accident on 14 May 1982. Peter's brother George then ran the property until he retired and his nephew, David, was old enough to take the reins.

David, the present day owner, (pictured above) is the fourth generation to farm the Pinckney kingdom, which today covers some 68 000ha of which 5450ha in the valley floor are freehold and the rest is leased from the Crown. Glenaray runs along the top of the Garvie Mountains (6000ft), with a 50km boundary with Nokomai Station to the west. It neighbours, Carrick, Cairnmuir and Earnscleugh to the north, Department of Conservation land, Gem Lake and Argyle Station to the east and Glenlapa and several smaller holdings to the south.

There are a few changes afoot on Glenaray,

FROM THISTLE TO FERN

David is moving from the traditional half-bred sheep, on the mid-altitude tussock country, to running Perendales. "There is more emphasis on meat production now so there are 15 000 Perendale ewes, with a quarter of them covered by terminal sires. The Perendales are more aggressive foragers – they control more gorse and broom than the half-breds," said David.

"We realise that the wool cheque will drop, but the cast ewes will be worth more than the half-breds and they are more prolific."

With a total sheep count of around 52 000, the 19 000 Romney ewe flock which graze the lower ground, including 1000ha of improved pasture make up the lions' share. On the high ground the wethers, which were historically a Merino/Romney cross, are now Merinos.

Each year 10 000 ewe hoggets are wintered for replacements and are strip fed on swedes and kale.

A major deer expansion, near completion, has been underway for the past three years. Initially, there was a velveting unit near the homestead, of some 200ha, which carried 500 stags and a further 1000 Red hinds were running on another 200ha block near Gow Burn. This block has been extended to run 4500 hinds on an extensive basis, set stocking and handling only once a year to reduce costs. "It is our long term intention to finish all our own deer. Presently we sell store. On the velvet front, we harvest 2.5-3kgs/hd annually, which is OK for a commercial herd but we are aiming higher."

Glenaray differs from the majority of high country stations in the way it is run – as a business with a board of directors. A complete annual budget is drawn up, business plan drafted and goals set. The station mission statement is: PLANNING – PEOPLE – COMMUNICATION. The board is chaired by George Pinckney (David's uncle) and includes: John Tavendale, Rodger Bonifart, Tom and David Pinckney.

David is the Managing Director and feels that making a point of interaction with his permanent staff of 15 is very important. He is constantly liasing with his management team: station manager, Horace Miller, East End Farm manager (finishing farm), Thames Prouchman and administration manager, Barbara Wilson.

All the beef and lamb from the station is finished on a 270ha property near Gore and goes direct to the meat works. "If the store markets are strong, we are quite flexible and may sell some – it is basically down to the best economic decision," said David.

"The cattle play a major role in pasture management by keeping the grass down to the right condition for sheep between Oct to March due to excessive growth during that period."

The 4440 head of Hereford cattle are made up of 1800 rising 3-year old cows, 1720 rising 2-year old heifers, 920 1-year old heifers. The 920 1-year old steers also run on the property before heading down country to the fattening unit. Some 43 bulls are used to cover the cattle, with a quarter being covered by Charolais sires.

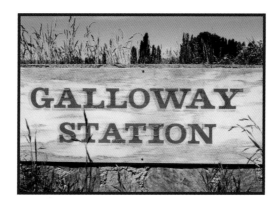

GALLOWAY STATION

There was brilliant sunshine and the temperature was beginning to rise dramatically as I headed towards Galloway Station, making my way out of the town of Alexandra, famed for its fruit growing and enormous 'clock on the rock'.

It was quite a contrast being led into the cool interior of the stone built homestead, dating back to 1865, by Andrew Preston who has been farming the property since 1982.

"I farm very much in a similar way to one hundred years ago," commented Andrew, as we sat at the kitchen table.

"The property is divided into three blocks: the front section is the winter country, the middle is the spring country and the back block, which is susceptible to large snow deposits, is used as the summer grazing," he explains.

"My grandfather, Harold Preston, came over from Scotland, I'm not sure from where and bought the Station in 1929."

The etymology of Galloway Station, as the name implies, hails from the Southwest region of Scotland, now referred to as Dumfries and Galloway. The Shennan brothers who claimed the original 160 000 acre (66 666ha) holding (Run No 220) in 1858, named their property after their homeland. Another brother, John took on Run No.221 which was originally named the Manuherikia run, but was renamed "Moutere". John gave up his land to his brother Watson after a year.

Watson Shennan and his brother Alexander sailed out from Scotland aboard the 'Thomas and Henry,' arriving in Dunedin in October 1857. Watson, the senior, was only twenty-two years old when they set inland on horseback, some three months later, searching for their 'Promised Land'. Their only guide was a basic Maori map, which merely bore the name of one river – the 'Manuherikia River.'

From the top of the Knobbies range, they choose a grassy, well-watered spot in the Manuherikia Valley, stretching from Oripu to Roxburgh. Apparently these pioneering lowland Scots were only the third white people to visit the Alexandra/Clyde area and the first to claim some land.

The Shennans set out from Balclutha on March 31, 1858 with a good line of ewes they had purchased for their run. The route over the Lammerlaw Mountains was chosen as the most practical droving course. It proved to be quite an expedition.

Firstly the party were held up, as the muddy terrain was not suited to the bullock wagon and dray so they substituted it with sledges. Then sheep, shepherds and horses were caught in a snow blizzard, with drifts ranging from four to thirty feet, which drew the journey out over a month.

In 1910, the 'Tapanui Courier' featured an account from Watson Shennan of conditions endured while droving sheep from the Tokomairiro to the Galloway and Moutere runs.

Mr Shennan began, *"The sheep journeyed on, with provisions carried on pack horses, but the progress was very slow on account of the rough nature of the country. They had to go over the highest part of the Lammerlaws, when one of the severest snowstorms imaginable caught them. What happened during the next three or four*

Woolshed near Alexandra.

Merinos on the move.

a terrible experience in the snow, and for over a week the mob could not be moved. They were practically under the snow, and were in deep snow for three weeks. The horses had to be moved from one big snow tussock to another that being the only food they could get. The party could only find enough sticks to boil the billy and cook a chop; not sufficient for a fire to warm them. A journey to the South Pole is nothing to a trip like that."

The Shennan brothers imported long wool sheep, from their homeland in 1859 and 1861 and also from the North Island, to enhance and develop their stock.

By 1860 Watson and Alexander had sold the 160 000 acre Galloway run to Englishman, William A Low. Instead they decided to focus on the Moutere run.

In 1861 Alexander Shennan travelled to England and then Germany in search of purebred Merinos. He purchased fifteen stud rams and twenty-seven stud ewes from the King Wilhem I of Prussia's Potsdam Stud and shipped them over to New Zealand along with two English Leicester rams. They cost the grand sum of two thousand pounds.

John Beattie, a young Scottish shepherd escorted the Stud Merinos on their voyage to New Zealand aboard the 'Oliver Cromwell'. On their arrival at Port Chalmers, on 7 April 1862, the Scot and his flock were transported into a smaller boat for the trip to Waikouaiti. The tide was high, so Maoris came and carried the foreign ovines and their keeper ashore as there was no quay at Waikouaiti.

These hardy young Scots were not only the first to have sheep in Central in 1858, but also the first to bring Merinos to Otago.

Alexander did not return from his overseas trip, instead he took a change of direction in his career and matriculated at Edinburgh University to study medicine. He died from Rheumatic fever in Edinburgh in 1863. Some reckon he had been subjected to too much hardship at such an

weeks would take more time and space to describe than the writer can afford. I will only say that I do not think it possible to experience greater hardship and live – especially that suffered by the party with the sheep; and having to change the dray for sledges caused much of the trouble.

The sheep (with my brother in charge) and the bullock teams, personally driven, got separated some forty miles by a mountain. The Lammerlaws were covered with snow, from four to thirty feet deep. The teams could not face this, and there was no way round. The party with the sheep I knew would be getting short of provisions, and that made me very anxious, as it was impossible to say what had happened to them if caught in the snow. It was necessary to push on, and I made two attempts, both times getting a long way up the mountain; but was driven back to lower ground by

fresh snowstorms. The third try was successful. Where the snow was deep it got frozen hard, and carried the bullocks and sledges, so my charge managed to get over. My party had nothing hot to eat or drink for three days, and the bullocks were not out of the yokes for the same time, and had hardly any food.

When I picked up the party with the sheep in Ida Valley, they were out of provisions, and had only mutton to eat for some days, and had lost a man and horse. The missing man had been sent back to bring up some stores that had been left behind, but he did not find the provisions and lost himself. After three days' search my brother managed to pick him up. He had had very little food, and I have never seen a man so hungry as he was; but we restricted him to small quantities of food for some days. The party with the sheep had

early age.

Watson lost the will for the station life and returned to Scotland, selling up lock, stock and barrel at Moutere before his departure. In six years, he came back to New Zealand, this time to the Maniototo, as owner of Puketoi. It was from this station that his Merino Stud received worldwide recognition.

Today Galloway Station is still synonymous with quality Merinos. Andrew runs 8200, of Merrivale Bloodlines, on the hill. This figure includes 2500 wethers, which are run on the back blocks of Raggedy Range, where paddocks vary in area from 400 hectares to 2250ha. This terrain can now be reached in two and a half hours in a 4-wheel drive.

We took a drive through the lower reaches of the property and then out on to the Range. The topography was a mix between a lunar landscape and a set off a wild-west movie. My imagination was running riot, half expecting to see Billy the Kid or Buckshot Roberts careering round one of the rocky outcrops.

To me, the hills looked stark, not unlike parts of Australia, minus the red tinge, and I wondered what on earth the sheep actually ate.

"The Merinos thrive in these conditions," said Andrew, as he pointed out the native grasses, "with only 330mm of rain a year we have no foot rot or wool problems to contend with."

"Hogget wool measures 17.8 micron and the adult ewes and wethers are usually between 19.1 and 19.3 micron, averaging 5.4kgs a fleece." (Wool of 19.2 micron and finer commands a premium in the market place.)

Peter Lyons, the largest shearing contractor in New Zealand, who has recently become Fernmark Quality accredited, sends a gang out to machine shear in the four stand shed at Galloway in September. Crutching is done in March. All wool samples are sent to a broker in Christchurch and are e-mailed to Hainsworth Mills in England.

They are pretty much easy care, cost effective, wool producing machines, as they require no supplementary feeding and only receive two drenches a year.

The first shearing at Galloway was in 1858, when the shearers were paid 15/- (shillings) for an eight hour day and three glasses of rum each. In these days the wool was sledged 130 miles to Waikouaiti, two bales at a time. It took Watson Shennan almost all the summer to shift the clip down country and supplies back.

Lunar landscape on Galloway above and the rams below a rocky outcrop.

SHEARING AT GALLOWAY

The shearing time has come again,
The cook is in the galley,
The learners here all mean to try
and beat the ringer's tally.

We're rather short of shearers yet,
We only have the two,
But when they're in the humour
They can shove out quite a few.

We've a slim wee chap works on the board,
He picks up all the fleeces,
By the time they reach the table
They're mostly all in pieces.

He's a ball of muscle most days,
He's as fit as any flea,
Just watch him jump to tar the place
Where the hind leg used to be.

There's two chaps at the table,
With their pinafores and shoes
They're just exactly what they look –
Two worn-out cockatoos.
There's a part time presser on the job
We'll mention in this rhyme,
He's a cockatoo from down the road
But he's not here all the time.

There's a shepherd works around the shed,
He's always in for lunch,
He's got a pack of mustering dogs
That seem a handy bunch.

Here comes the boss, we know his step,
"Well boys, the sheep are tough,
You're shoving out the tallies
But you're getting mighty rough.

"You squeal for higher wages
And you'd take it every one,
And yet you're sending half my wool

Out upon the run."

And when the smoko comes along
They sit round on the bales,
They entertain each other
Telling funny tales.

The tales are very funny
When you hear them tell them right,
There's other ones quite good to hear
That you really wouldn't write.

The boss says in his pleasant way
As he gives a little cough,
"My sheep won't get rheumatics
If you take the stockings off."

I've seen some woolsheds in my time
And I've worked in quite a few,
But Galloway seems quite different –
Each man's a cockatoo.
Anonymous

Prior to the 1894 Arbitration and Conciliation Act, Stations drew up their own agreements with staff, shearers and shed hands. On Galloway and Teviot Stations, the following rules were laid out: *"Smoking shall only be allowed at the recognised intervals of work and neither smoking nor spitting shall be permitted when at work in the shed or at the shearing board. No obscene language shall be allowed nor shall unnecessary noises or disturbances be made in the shed. Persistence in such conduct will render the persons liable to summary dismissal."* Singing was also banned in the shed hand's agreement.

Sounds like a bundle of laughs! Wonder what they would have made of the ghetto blasters and sounds of today. But I must agree that the smoking ban is a great idea. While shearing, I can always tell when someone has lit up in the shed – not sure if it is because a woman uses a smaller amount of lung capacity, that I am so aware and abhor anyone smoking anywhere near me while pushing a handpiece.

Rams on Galloway group together to try and get some shelter from the sun.

GALLOWAY STATION

Plenty of poetry seems have to been written about Galloway Station – this one, by George Meek reflects the Agreement above.

SHEDS THAT BANNED THE SINGING
ROUSEY'S SONG

When you're rolling up fleeces,
Skirting off the daggy pieces,
Keep your head and don't start warbling of the
home you left outback;
Should you strike a big fat thistle,
And forget yourself and whistle –
If the blinkin' boss is hangin' round, you're next
for down the track.

When around the boss is prowling,
With a face all sour, and scowling,
And you fancy you can hear your best girl singing,
"Smile boys Smile;"
Don't get serenading Hilda,
Or next morning with Matilda –
You'll be singing down the road with bonnie
Mary of Argyle.

When you're tying up the fleeces,
Should your wool rope snap to pieces,
And you feel you'd like to let her go and swear like
Merry hell;
Keep as cool as a cucumber,
Or tomorrow night you'll slumber
Underneath a cocky's haystack – certainly not the
Grand Hotel.

While the shearers croon their swear theme –
Let the boss in silence blaspheme –
Carry on! It's all a part in life's human mystery
play;
When sky prices wool is bringing,
The old bosses will be singing
Of the old shed hands and shearers, who helped them
prepare the way.

When the tory starts to totter,
You might be a full-blown squatter,
Driving up and down the country with a pair of
spanking bays;
And your woolshed will be ringing
With the rousey's chorus singing
Of old Galloway and Teviot in the good old station days.

Rocky outcrops and Dog Rock on Galloway Station.

The new Galloway owner, William A Low, who also owned and operated Run No 256 – Cairn Hill, went into partnership with property tycoon, Robert Campbell, shortly after taking on the station, due to financial difficulties. They jointly purchased Benmore Station near Omarama in 1863.

His wife, daughter of Dunedin Doctor Andrew Buchanan, designed the present day homestead, which was erected in 1865. The twelve bed-roomed house, with 600mm stone exterior walls and cob divisions inside, replaced the Shennan's clay walled, flax roofed abode. She wanted the family home to be warm in winter and cool in summer. She succeeded – as it was lovely and cool during my visit! The stables, chaff house and single men's quarters were all built in the same fashion and are a testament to her skill as an Architect.

Low was considered a fair and lenient boss. On one occasion he was following a ridge, one of the station boundaries, when he came across a horse with its' rider asleep nearby in the tussock. When asked for general directions, the boundary keeper merely stabbed a toe in the direction of Black's run at Lauder. "Is that all the courtesy you can show a traveller?" Low enquired before he set off on his way.

In the early days of run holding, before fencing was undertaken, men were employed as boundary keepers to ensure that the sheep did not wander and remained within the property borders.

Another keeper was playing billiards in an Alexandra alehouse when he was asked by Low who he was. The gent in question replied that he was a boundary keeper from Galloway Station. To which Low replied, "And I suppose this is your boundary?" Both men were very lucky to keep their positions.

In 1878, Low sold his shares to partner, Robert Campbell, who then employed a series of managers until subdivision in 1916. The first manager taken on at Galloway was in the form of

The Galloway Homestead and some of the original out houses.

GALLOWAY STATION

William Gilbert Rees (born in North Wales, April 1827). He had secured a run in his own right on the shores of Lake Wakatipu, where Queenstown now stands, but gold was found and he had to relinquish his lease.

Rees settled down here on this nice quiet station,
The Lake was a scene then of calm desolation;
He'd cross the Shotover his cattle to find,
But that nuggets lay there never entered his mind
His shepherd then daily unconsciously trod
Over tons of bright gold lying hid in the sod,
And Rees drove in bullocks and branded away,
Never thinking what money they'd fetch him some day.
So just look around and you'll quickly behold
The wonderful changes effected by gold;
We keep shifting about, and a fellows' perplexed,
The question is, "Where will we have to rush to next."

Thatcher

Robert Gunion took the helm from 1883 to 1896, followed by J. Tait and D. Rose who managed the property for a few months each. Alex Gunn, whose son Davy had the Hollyford, arrived in 1896 and remained there until Galloway was subdivided in 1916 into six blocks: Little Valley, Matangi, Riverside, Crawfords, The Goulburn and Mount Campbell.

The homestead block today stands at 11 500 hectares (28000 acres), less than a fifth of the size of the mighty run taken up by the Shennans 142 years ago. It was purchased by the Elliots shortly after subdivision, and was soon sold to the Spain family of nearby Earnscleugh Station who held it until 1929 when Andrew Preston's grandfather, Harold, bought it.

As the third generation of Prestons to farm at Galloway, Andrew has made several changes. Cattle were introduced to the property for the first time in 1983. He had been running 120 Hereford cattle, covered by a Charolais bull, but due to the drought of 1999 he sold them last year.

Andrew is now focusing his efforts on a deer enterprise, with over 200 hectares already deer fenced and a view to expand onto the hill. Presently 700 Red deer hinds and 150 stags are at large. A Wapiti stag is used to cover the hinds to increase live weights and hybrid vigour. Most stags used are of Warnham Bloodlines.

"Red deer are not so susceptible to worms," he stated, "they are grazed mostly on flood irrigated land."

The weaners are all finished on farm, with potential velveters kept. "The 2 year olds on average cut 2.5 – 3kgs of velvet and the 3 year olds, 3-4.7kgs."

The property is run extensively and stocked conservatively.

Two men are employed: Glen is more or less full time on the deer enterprise and Garry is the rabbiter and poisons possums as well. Mustering is done on a casual basis on foot.

In his spare time, mainly between April and September, when things are not so busy at Galloway, Andrew follows his passion for hunting and works as a hunting guide. He operates in partnership with another guide, who organises most of their customers. The clients, who are mainly Americans, come across to hunt the wild pigs, deer, chamois and thar in the New Zealand hinterland.

Andrew is the proud owner of a Mauke – a short take off and landing aircraft. The property also boasts a shooting range, which is used by the police for target practice.

Some of the Galloway sheep being sold at the Cromwell Saleyards.

Gateway to Galloway

MOUNT LINTON REVISITED

Two weeks after my trip to Mount Linton I met up with the staff at the Mossburn Hack Races on the sun drenched, windswept plains at Branxton Hill. The station had the strongest contingent at the event running twelve horses out of the forty entered.

Stock manager Bart Sherbourne outpaced the pack in the walk, trot, gallop and saddle trot races, securing a further two seconds and a third to come third overall on the scoreboard. On the other hand, the gardener – John O'Leary – trotted to victory in the harness race, with another three placings to his credit.

The cross-country course was the highlight of the day, with an awesome 2.4m deep water hole which competing horses had to swim through before the final gallop home to the finish line. As reporter for the local newspaper, the banks of the water jump made an ideal spot for action shots of soaking steeds and their riders.

At the Invercargill Rodeo the following day, I spent most of the time in a ute (pickup) writing up my copy on the races and Riversdale Shears. Some of the shepherds were riding the bulls and they had put my name down for the female steer ride. I was thanking my lucky stars that due to some unforseen circumstances the steers had not arrived at the venue!

Shearing was due to start at Mount Linton in a couple of week's time so I phoned the local contractor – Jim Malcolm of Western Southland Shearing to see if there was any chance of a stand, in the impressive 12 stand wool shed. I thought it would be a good financial back up as I was still a bit wary of earning a living full time from journalism.

Sometimes it is pretty hard as a female shearer to be taken seriously, but Jim Malcolm listened intently as I explained that I was over from Scotland, was writing a book on the sheep stations established by Scotsmen and wondered if he would consider giving me a stand shearing at Mount Linton for three weeks.

"Come and see me in the next couple of days when the weather clears up and we'll give you a go," he replied.

Dutifully I turned up at the quarters in Ohai to meet Mr Malcolm. He was a big man with a warm smile and a good grip of New Zealand in his handshake. "My grandfather, Alexander Malcolm came out from Inverness and we still have his kilt," he proudly announced.

He showed me round the quarters, leading the way down long dark corridors, to a spartan but spotless room, which was well positioned opposite the ladies showers and toilets. The grinding room was the next port of call. It was very dark with smoke belching seemingly out of the brickwork. I later found that the boiler was next door. The laundry facilities and shearing/general stores shop were next on the agenda. Finally we ended up in the dining room where two cheery cooks dished up a feed fit for a

Eleven thousand sheep on the run!

Sumo Wrestler. I did my best, but could hardly make a dent in the mountain of food.

As it was still raining, Mr Malcolm said that I could move in immediately or keep in touch until things dried up.

A couple of days later it was all go at the station front. I was quite excited as I carried my gear up the steep steps into the wool shed, at getting the chance to shear in such a large gang. The average shed in Southland has three or four stands and I was finally managing to fulfil two of my pipedreams in one fell swoop: shearing on a station and in a big shed.

The contractor that I used to work for, Trevor Middleton of Hokonui said that in his day Mount Linton Station shearing shed was by invitation only. All the top shearers from around the district from different gangs were hand picked to fill the stands and it was an honour to be asked.

I suppose after eight years of shearing across Scotland, Australia, New Zealand and England I have become used to being stared at, when I first enter a shed. Most people have the preconceived idea that a female shearer will have some butch hair do and be built like a tank – I like to surprise them!

Every one was really friendly, introducing themselves, but some of the shearers hung back, probably waiting to see what this chick could do on the boards. One of the rousies actually told me afterwards that a couple of the guys were quite concerned about having their street credit ruined by being beaten by a woman! They had nothing to worry about – I was pretty unfit.

In my time I have worked with heaps of guys in the shearing world and in other agricultural fields and only very occasionally I have come up against sexism and prejudice. On the shearing competition circuit some guys cannot contain themselves, when beaten in the semi finals or finals, in a male dominated sport, by the fairer sex. But on the whole, the majority of shearers that I have shorn with have been absolute gentlemen and those with whom I worked at Mount Linton were no exception. In fact they couldn't have been better, taking time off their stands to help me with my borrowed gear and showing me some moves and footwork to quicken my pace on the lambs.

Stand six, midway down the board was my posting for the first week. Each shearer had the usual individual catching pens and portholes, which were like the black hole of Calcutta as the shed was so high.

We started on lambs – a bit of a shock to the system, but they are not so hard on the body. At the days end one is not so physically exhausted from dragging out the lighter live weight.

Cover combs were in force to leave a little extra wool on the lambs. This was a bit of a novelty for me in more ways than one – I'd never used a cover comb and hadn't shorn lambs for about five years. Since August 1994, I have only done the UK summer shearing season, which lasts a maximum of three months, as it tied in with

This photo of Scottie made the front cover of the Southland Times!

Bart Sherbourne goes for gold in the water.

other work commitments.

To cut a long story short, this time, I was basically going into shearing cold and unfit. After a few tense movements round the back legs, having been warned at how easy it was to hamstring a lamb with a cover comb and trying to remember all the extra blows around the head, to remove the Kiwi 'facial hair' – I relaxed a bit more and let the handpiece flow.

There were some colourful characters working in the gang, some with a lifetime behind the handpiece, others just learning. I was surprised at how old some of them were: Percy and Boy both in their sixties. Regardless that I was female, foreign and Pakeha, a bit of a novelty I suppose, I was accepted as one of the crew.

At one point I was aware that some of the station staff were watching, so I was sweeping up the long blow, trying to impress, when my down tube seemed to loose power. I then realised that Johnny, the station truckie, was up to his pranks again – he had pulled the fuse for my machine out of the box at the end of the board, much to everyone's amusement, most of all, his own! He's probably the jolliest chap I've ever met, wearing a permanent grin on his face.

Sometimes Glenn Prebble or Robert Grant, the shepherds, or Bart the stock manager would come and shear one for me during my first week. Some of the shearers were great, taking time off their stands to give me a few pointers in the art of lamb shearing and contractor, Jim Malcolm, also spent some time on my stand, in an advisory capacity.

It was quite a blessing to get onto the ewes – I was handling as many ewes an hour as lambs! Incidentally, I was managing to almost finish the Sumo Wrestler portions each evening and must add, as far as quarters go, the food was first class.

In the second week, I was shifted to stand two, not sure if it was promotion or not – maybe it was to give me go faster stripes, as I now had the ganger, Darren Murray behind me popping out 400 a day and Joe Edwards just in front on 401. It was probably to make things a bit easier on the rousies, who were working on two shearers apiece. At least they weren't twoing me – doing two to my every one!

Historically all the sheep on the Macgregor's run were Romneys, but as World wool prices have slipped, Texels have been introduced to

Jim Malcolm (in check shirt) and the gang I worked with for six weeks in the Mount Linton Shed.

improve carcass conformation and finishing weights (15.5-17kgs for the export market) as lamb is now the main earner on the property. Forty thousand ewes are still purebred Romneys with another twenty thousand being first cross to a Texel. These crossbreds have proved to be very hardy thriving on the hill, requiring no supplementary feeding.

Presently trials are being done using Finn and East Friesian terminal sires over the Romney x Texel ewes, to find the optimum meat lamb and assist ewe fecundity.

Two shearing sheds, one 12 stand and a 6 stand are used to relieve the 60 000 sheep of their fleeces. The station employs a wool buyer, who not only classes the wool in the shed at shearing, but deals direct with sixteen exporters, thus cutting out the middle man, selling above market average and increasing returns.

Mount Linton is considered one of New Zealand's leading sheep stations, always to the forefront of any national improvement trials or projects. General manager, Paul McCarthy, instigated and chairs a research group for upgrading hill country as well as heading the Otago/Southland Sheep Council, which is presently running trials for possible causes of bearings (prolapses) in ewes.

Back at the quarters everyone was woken for breakfast at 5am, which was a bit of a shock to the system. Most shearers had a full fried breakfast with all the trimmings, but I opted for a couple of pieces of toast and a cup of tea, as I'm not really a morning person. After breakfast we grabbed our gear and waited for our ganger (the one who is in charge in the shed, if there are any problems and also keeps a record of all the tallies and shed hands hours) to drive round in a minibus. It was a bit of a commotion, like a bus stop. Everyone checked the notice board after 6pm the previous evening to see if they were working, being listed under each ganger and the shed where they were going. I always tried to spot someone who was in my gang and get on the same bus.

Jim Malcolm runs about 7 or 8 gangs at the height of the season, so one can imagine the organization involved in ensuring that everyone knew where they were going, had their gear and the vans were loaded with the required amount of food for two smokos and lunch for the day.

Shearing on stand six half way down the shed.

Full sheep yards at the Kyeburn woolshed.

KYEBURN STATION

It was a dreich, miserable, grey day when I drove into Kyeburn Station, in the heart of the Maniototo, but there was a hive of activity around the homestead and the yards were just buzzing. Nicolas Mackenzie had told me the night before to turn up regardless as the lads were arriving home form the annual muster accompanied by the Country Calendar TV film crew and I should be able to get plenty action shots.

The Kyeburn woolshed, shearing quarters and outhouses stood out as they were all painted white with red trim. As shearing sheds go this one is more architecturally pleasing to the eye than most run of the mill corrugated iron or wooden sheds. The dormer windows reminded me of Scottish croft houses and the raised turret, which was added to house the wool press, was another attractive feature. From a shearers' point of view, it probably wasn't as flash as the board was a really wide drag across so would require more physical exertion than most!

Out in the yards the men were busy drafting sheep, as some of the neighbouring high country is used, as in the Scottish Highlands, for common grazing. This is where several sheep owners graze their flocks on the same area of land but have individual earmarks. Here in the Maniototo the common land is only used as summer grazing, with the sheep being brought down to their respective holdings for the winter months.

The musterers, clad in driza bones, Swannies and other wet weather gear, were tired after their ten day stint on the hills and in some cases, they over indulged in alcohol during the evening gatherings in the huts.

Just before lunch Mr Mackenzie took me into the farmhouse to meet his wife, who seemed delighted at the prospect of some female help. She was frantically running round the kitchen in anticipation of serving up a three-course lunch for twenty-two hungry men. I got stuck in and assisted her by dolloping potatoes and vegetables onto numerous plates, passing them round then picking up dirty dishes in preparation for the next sitting.

Mid afternoon, while the shepherds were still sorting out the mobs, I was taken on a tour of the low ground on the property by Nicholas, who has run Kyeburn since 1968. He along with son Hamish, who has returned from a stint overseas, are developing the property to its full potential, reseeding and using winter crops to their advantage.

That evening once the musterers had moved off with their mobs of sheep or retired for the evening, the film crew had stopped the cameras rolling and every last dish had been through the washer, Nicolas, his wife and son Hamish sat down with me to discuss the history of the property over a stiff drink.

John Barton and Alexander McMaster originally held Kyeburn Station, the name 'kye' being lowland Scots for 'cattle' or cows, from 5 September 1858. This 49 000ha holding ran from Kokonga to Naseby, over the Hawkdun Ranges to the Otematata River and Danseys Pass.

By April 1866 the property was on the

market, with 17 500 sheep and sold for $20 000 to William Sanders, of Dumfriesshire, Scotland, latterly Victoria, Australia. This purchase was for the 10 828ha Upper Kyeburn – run 211 and for a seventeen-year lease of the 16 920ha Mount Buster – run 362. Saunders also secured 7500ha of the low ground for a 16 year period, while Barton and McMaster kept the remainder - 206B – to be worked with their runs over the range. This latter arrangement did not work and that

land is now farmed by three different concerns: Shortland, Sunset Farm and Clover Flat.

The nearby village of Naseby was renowned for its gold diggings, but nowadays is probably more famed for the Scottish sport of curling. As the gold prospects dried up, the miners opted for farming and eventually won the lowland run 206, amounting to 2015ha of the original Kyeburn Station.

In June 1875 'Mackenzie of Deep Dell', Macraes, purchased the then 26 796ha Kyeburn from Sanders for $36 000, the deal including 42 000 sheep. The Mackenzie in question was

Mount Ida Syndicate and was the one, which had been mustered during my visit.

Apparently Sanders returned to Scotland and toured Europe with Watson Shennan, of Galloway Station. He then went to stay with his brother Robert, the minister of Thundergarth in Dumfriesshire and purchased a farm – Rosebank. Four years later he was back in New Zealand, the North Island this time, where he bought Motouotaraia in Hawkes Bay. His nephew

managing Deep Dell Station, Otago, New Zealand.

At Deep Dell Scobie developed his writing skills and regularly contributed to the New Zealand Magazine, Otago Witness and Mt Ida Chronicle and was also involved in politics. His partners: Stewart and Rich were a retired banker and a stud breeder respectively. Scobie bought his partners out around 1888 and the land was leased out.

Scobie Mackenzie died in 1901 and his widow,

Jessy Adela (nee Bell) kept the property on till her death in 1937 when it was passed to her son, Alexander Kenneth Scobie Mackenzie, who was a Wellington based lawyer. It was run by a succession of managers till Nicolas Scobie Mackenzie, a great grandson of the original Scobie, took over the management in 1968.

In 1918 Kyeburn was divided for soldier settlement and the stations: Allan Peaks, Idavale and Glenshee were born. Kyeburn also lost some of the high country at this juncture for summer grazing for the new low ground properties. This 4925ha

Mackay John Scobie Mackenzie, who invested in Kyeburn in cahoots with Francis Dyer Rich and Charles Stewart.
Sanders and his agent J.M Ritchie had decided that the balance between summer and winter grazing was uneven on the original Kyeburn Station so the most distant 6430 ha were sold to the Mount Ida Pastoral & Investment Company who also farmed Rugged Ridges, Eweburn and Eden Creek. This block is now part of the

Robert Johnstone, who had been employed on Kyeburn and Conical Hills was installed as manager and eventually bought it from his uncle, when he returned to Scotland.

Scobie Mackenzie was born in Tain in January 1845 and was well educated at Tain Acadamey and Watson's in Edinburgh, before emigrating to Australia with his mother and siblings. At sixteen he was employed on a station and eventually became a manager. He was then offered a post

block is known as the Soldiers' Syndicate and is positioned next to the Mount Ida Syndicate.

Kyeburn was probably the last station to still use a team of mules for carting the gear from one hut to another on the musters. Apparently the first donkey arrived on the station from Otekaieke Station in 1896. They were noted for their hardiness, requiring no supplementary feeding or shoes.

Shepherds from the Mount Ida Syndicate.

Inside the Kyeburn woolshed – an overhead drive shaft and drag across board.

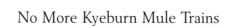

No More Kyeburn Mule Trains

They say its four-wheel drive now on a bulldozed road and all,
And the Pack Horse Bend and Lone Mule Creek are names beyond recall.
Busted Diff and Broken Axle, Punctured Tyre and Blowout Point
Are the new names through the ranges – but my heart feels out of joint.
McMillan

You've got mail!

Nick MacKenzie, Kyeburn

Sheep all drafted and off to their respectie homes.

MACKENZIE COUNTRY

From the lonely sheiling of the misty island,
Mountains divide us and a waste of seas,
Yet still the blood is strong, the heart is Highland,
And we in our dreams behold the Hebrides.

In the heart of the High Country, in the South Island, lies an area called the Mackenzie Country. Until 1855 it was uncharted territory. The early South Canterbury settlers were unaware that beyond the Snowy Ranges lay tremendous sheep country – a vast tussocky plain, crossed with rivers with glacial waters flowing into amazing blue azure lakes.

It was, the now legendary sheep stealer, James Mackenzie, born in Ross-shire, Scotland who discovered a pass and repeatedly secreted acquired mobs of sheep via this route, across the plains of the hinterland and beyond.

The Rhodes brothers were the first to settle in South Canterbury when they moved a mob of 5000 sheep from their Banks Peninsula property, near Christchurch to the 60 000ha Levels Station in June 1851. By 1855 there were 24 000 sheep on the Levels.

In these days sheep were tended by boundary keepers staying in back country huts. Apparently the two Maoris – Taiko and Seventeen – in charge of the Levels sheep were more prone to playing cards in the huts than tending the sheep, making easy pickings for Mackenzie. Completely by chance a young lad sent to find the station horses spotted James Mackenzie, his dog 'Friday' and his bullock used for packing making off with a mob of sheep.

The lad returned to the station and reported to the manager – John Sidebottom – what he had seen. The following day Sidebottom, Taiko and Seventeen set out in hot pursuit. After a couple of days tracking they came upon the Scottish sheep stealer, his dog, bullock and the stolen flock. A tussle ensued and the thieving Highlander was arrested.

Sidebottom decided to head back with the sheep immediately but thick fog came down and Mackenzie managed to escape, leaving his bullock, dog and the sheep behind. He was recaptured, some days later, in a loft in the port of Lyttelton where he was waiting to board a ship to escape.

The Lyttelton Times, dated 18 April, reported

that: "The prisoner endeavoured to evade the responsibility of crime by pretending not to understand the English language, and he occasionally gesticulated in Gaelic, but upon the empanelling of a jury to decide whether he was really ignorant of the language, several witnesses proved that they had conversed with him in English, which, at those times, he appeared to understand perfectly. The jury decided the prisoner was guilty of 'mute of malice', when the judge directed a plea of 'not guilty on the charge of robbery' to be recorded and the trial proceeded."

The verdict found Mackenzie guilty and he was sentenced to five years imprisonment and hard labour. This red haired rogue managed to escape not just once but three times; firstly while labouring, a couple of months later from the prison still in leg irons and then again from a labouring gang.

Eventually (Jan 1856) Mackenzie was pardoned by the Governor, Henry J Tranced, on condition that he left the country immediately.

Deer on Braemar Station, MacKenzie Country.

Tranced had written a report, to which the Superintendent of Canterbury had added '..I am quite satisfied that although he does understand English, he both speaks and understands it with great difficulty when under any excitement." He paid his passage to Australia and that was the last sight or sound of James Mackenzie the now famous sheep stealer of the Mackenzie Country.

From that point on pioneers snapped up vast tracts of the Mackenzie Country for sheep stations, as had already been done throughout South Canterbury. Initially the run holders were English (Sassenachs), but due to the extremes of climate (Sahara type summers to Baltic winters), high winds and isolation, the Poms moved to warmer, more populated climes and left the Mackenzie Country to the Scottish shepherds. These hardy souls, brought up in windswept glens and heather clad slopes of the Highlands, were well accustomed to severe weather conditions and their canine cohorts – the collie dogs were used to operating on similar terrain and working at distance from their masters. Around 80% of

the inhabitants were Scottish with the majority being Gaelic speaking.

To this day the area still has a Highland air with the skirl of the pipes, kilts worn at functions, highland gatherings and the names: Burnett, Cameron, Mackenzie, Murray and Urquhart are still household entities on Mackenzie stations.

Several memorials stand testimony to the pioneers of the Mackenzie Country: the Church of St David (patron saint of shepherds) at Cave, The Church of the Good Shepherd on the shores of Lake Tekapo with a bronze statue of a collie dog nearby – inscribed "Beannachdan air na cu caorach." (Blessings on the sheep dogs) A large three-sided slab of Timaru bluestone marks the spot where James Mackenzie was first captured. On it in English, Gaelic and Maori is the inscription: "In this spot James Mackenzie, the freebooter, was captured by John Sidebottom and the Maoris 'Taiko' and 'Seventeen' and escaped from them the same night, March 4, 1855."

James Mackenzie also apparently caused a

Hamish MacKenzie and dogs, Braemar Station.

commotion in Aberdeenshire before he emigrated. The story goes that as a drover and cattle dealer he was requested to provide beef for the Lord Provost to mark some great occasion in Aberdeen. Mackenzie stole the beasts from the Lord Provost's estate, delivered them, collected his money and vanished before the misdemeanour was discovered. Many suspected the reiver had taken off to Australia.

Mackenzie had a marvellous dog,
Named Friday, full of knowing;
She never barked while working sheep
With slinking grace, eyes glowing.

And as they went from Lyttelton
Towards the snow peaked hills,
They looked for sheep to steal, it's said
At night by Friday's skills.

Man and dog roamed Canterbury,
The land too dear to settle.
By chance they found a mountain pass
And plains to test their mettle –

Three hundred miles of tussock grasses,
Thorn-scrub, river torrents.
The witch-dog set the travelling pace,
They crossed Otago Province.

―――

A sudden pounce – and Jock was caught,
Sidebottom tied the dog,
His stockman claimed the stolen sheep….
Jock escaped in fog.

The hunt was on; at Lyttelton
Seager caught him sleeping.
Locked him in a stinking cell
With rats, and water seeping.
His trial in English muddled him,
The angry courtroom simmered.
When someone shouted "Hang the bitch,"
With tears his cheekbones glimmered.

The judge said he must clear himself.
No one spoke in favour.
Verdict: guilty. Sentence passed:
Five years, with hard labour.

No dog allowed, nor Gaelic Bible,
Heavy leg irons tired him,
He made escapes to find his dog,
Was caught….now folks admired him.

But some believed his trial unfair,
The evidence put badly.
When Tranced sought a pardon free,
The Governor signed it gladly.

T'wards midnight when the moon and stars
Conspired to hide their light,
They set him free from prison chains
To vanish from all sight.

Who knows if Jock did find his dog?
Or where their bones are lying?
Mackenzie Country is still the haunt
Of both their spirits sighing.
                    Diane and Gary Hebley

Tribute to John MacKenzie the sheep rustler - in English, Gaelic and Maori.

Bronze monument in recognition of the collie dog, Lake Tekapo, High Country

Lake Aviemore

Woolshed Ben Ohau Station, Twizel

BEN OHAU
STATION

Sheep on Ben Omar

Two Scotsmen: Alexander McMurdo and Hugh Fraser, who both managed properties in the Nelson area, to the North of the South Island, were the first to drive stock from there to new holdings in the Mackenzie Country in the 1850's.

On reaching the Ohau river, in the Mackenzie Country, these pioneering Scotsmen admired the sunny north-facing slopes above and apparently simultaneously exclaimed: 'I will have that country'. Instead of making off to the Christchurch Land Office to lay their claims, they decided to race to a matagouri bush to see who would take up the land. McMurdo was victorious and landed Benmore, Fraser took neighbouring Ben Ohau instead.

THE RACE FOR BENMORE STATION

Way at the back of Fairlie, beneath the Great Divide,
In the land found by Mackenzie, a million acres wide.
Last of the frontier country, lonely and apart,
A sea of golden tussock, with the iron in its heart.

Right on the farthest rim, hard by the mountain wall,
Stood a brace of mighty stations in the foremost rank of all.
One was named Ben Ohau, below the Ohau Range,
The other was called Benmore, vast, remote and strange.

They tell a famous story of how the land was won,
A cameo of history, a legend of the run.
Back in the 1850's, first of a rugged band,
Fraser and McMurdo came to this silent land.

Two hundred thousand acres, rough, untouched, untamed,
Awaiting the pioneer, undiscovered and unclaimed.
Both set their hearts on Benmore, the larger of the pair,
Though beautiful Ben Ohau was every bit as fair.

They settled the matter quickly, as men of action will,
A match-race for the choice, to the foot of a distant hill.
Each man was well-mounted, on a splendid rangy steed,
Tough and strong and game, built for guts and speed.

At the crack of Fraser's pistol, they flew out from the mark,
By the grandstand of the mountains, magnificent and stark.
Fighting for their heads, alive with speed and grace,
Bellies brushing tussock, they settled to the race.

Sods and gravel spurted beneath the flying pair,
And clouds of yellow dust, hung in the sunlit air.
Seven furlongs covered, and neither broke the line,
Though Fraser showed out slightly, coming to the nine.

The lead was just a whisker, and dearly was it bought,
The more he tried to stretch it, the more McMurdo fought.
Roaring up a gully they hit the rolling crest,
To face an ugly chasm, reaching to the west.

Too late to pull up short, too late to swing away,
The only path was forward, the only hope was pray.
Like blooded steeplechasers, in one almighty bound,
They cleared the yawning gulf, and both made good their ground.

Forward, ever forward, with barely slackened pace,
The drum-roll of their passage filled that silent place.
A clump of matagouri leaping into view,
Was ripped apart like paper, as they strongly barrelled through.

Fraser's hat went flying, his horse threw off a shoe,
McMurdo's saddle slipped, and his bridle snapped in two.
In and out of creek beds, up and down the banks,
They drove the snorting chargers, with foam-caked bloody flanks.

Onward, onward, onward, over the stony plain,
Rash and reckless riding, a glittering prize to gain.
Fraser held his margin, half a length in front,
McMurdo dropping back, but still there in the hunt.

Rising in his stirrups he saw the winning post,
A bunch of stunted bushes, a hundred yards at most.
Driving in his spurs, he let the horse fly free,
Roaring, raving, cursing, prayers and profanity.

Like a greyhound from the traps, like a bullet from a gun,
McMurdo's mighty chestnut made its final run.
A dozen giant strides just buried Fraser's grey,
McMurdo hit the front and McMurdo won the day.

Brian Barry

By April 1857 Hugh Fraser had taken up Run 179, while his brother Samuel took the adjoining Run 180. Runs 300, 319 and 327 were added to make the station, lying in the forks of the Pukaki and Ohau rivers, cover 60 515 acres in total. Samuel Fraser managed the property from 1858 till 1865 when Lachie McDonald took the post.

The Fraser's cultivated one acre of barley annually by hand, from which they distilled their own whisky. The Haldon Station diary, dated 22 August 1868, has an entry stating that they had received one gallon of whisky from the Fraser's of Ben Ohau.

The name 'Ben Ohau' is thought by some to come from the Gaelic – 'Beinn A'chu' meaning 'Mountain of the dogs', but others say that the Maoris and early settlers called it Lake 'Ohou'.

After a nine-month period on Ben Ohau, Hugh applied for another run – Black Forest Station – on 23 January 1858. This property lay to the North of the Waitaki River, now Lake Benmore since the damming of the Waitaki.

It was on Black Forest Station that the first recorded sheep dog trails took place. On 3 February 1869 the Timaru Herald reports, "The first of what is to be hoped will be an annual trial of sheepdogs, took place on Friday last on Mr Fraser's run, Black Forest, Mackenzie country. The conditions of the trial were to put three sheep into three separate pens in half an hour, the sheep having half a mile start." Hugh Fraser won the inaugural event with 'Black'. Mackenzie's 'Check', Mackay's 'Boy' and H. Fraser's 'Plato' were also placed.

The following year, the "Mackenzie Sweepstake" and the "Mt Cook Stakes" were up for grabs and a new event, which entailed hunting six sheep half a mile between sets of flags twenty yards apart at an angle of 45° was introduced, now named the 'Zig Zag Hunt'. J. McDonald and 'Bob' of Black Forest were victorious.

The Inverness-shire Highlander, from the Clan Fraser, also owned 900 acres at Raincliff, a 720 acre Balnacraig property near the Levels and 100 acres at Timaru, sold out everything in the early 1870's.

William Henry Ostler, Henry Dawson and Robert Campbell purchased Ben Ohau in 1867. Dawson who had managed Benmore for Campbell moved across the river to run Ben Ohau and Ostler took the managing position on Benmore.

Ostler, a large, red headed, Yorkshire man, bought out his partners in 1874 and farmed Ben Ohau till he died as a result of heart strain. The woolclip from the station crossed the Ohau River by means of a cage suspended from a wire rope, handling four bales at once. The cage would slide across the wire to the other side, similar to a flying fox. One bale slipped and was hanging precariously above the water, so Ostler hauled it in with the bale hook, but the strain was too much. It caused internal bleeding and he was

The Ben Ohau hill ground with a hydro canal in the foreground.

FROM THISTLE TO FERN

Simon Cameron, Ben Ohau Station owner.

found dead the next morning.

Mrs Ostler struggled financially, as sheep losses the previous winter had been extreme and the flock had to be restocked. The station was put up for auction and Goldsborough Mort and Company bought it in 1880 for below the mortgage price, installing William Stronach as manager.

Ben Ohau changed hands again in 1891, this time to James Preston, of Longlands and Fortrose Stations, Central Otago, whose descendants still have the property today, some 109 years on. Preston also owned Haldon and Black Forest Stations in the Mackenzie and financially assisted his brother-in-law, William Pringle, into Lilybank Station. Again in 1895 severe weather had struck Ben Ohau and Preston was considering selling….

Enter the Cameron saga…. The Cameron family who are now farming Ben Ohau have had their roots traced back as far as 1799 when Hugh Cameron of Styx, Aberfeldy, Perthshire, Scotland was married to Catherine Anderson. He (Hugh) was possibly the youngest of six, born to James and Isabel (nee Menzies) who wed in the parish of Dull 7/12/1757.

The Cameron's were tenants on the Breadalbane Estate, Aberfeldy and Kenmore and according to the 1841 Census Hugh was also a mason. Hugh and Catherine had five sons: James (20/12/1800) Donald (13/01/1802), John (21/10/1804), Alexander (7/07/1807) and Duncan (6/07/1810).

James the eldest was married on June 8th 1835, by the Rev. Edward Hume of Pitsligo, Aberdeenshire to Jane Keddie, daughter of James (a draper) and Jean (nee Steel). The couple spent the first twelve years of their married life managing the Tontine Hotel for the Tweedale Shooting Club. They then farmed at Innerleithen and then moved to the Island of Kerrera, off Oban, Argyllshire, where James purchased a farm – 'Ardentrive' in 1843.

James and Jane had seven children – 3 daughters and 4 sons:

Jane	born Peebles	(04/07/1836)
Catherine Ann	" "	(25/02/1838)
Hugh	" "	(13/11/1839)
James Keddie	" "	(10/06/1841)
John	Innerleithen	(04/12/1843)
Isabella McArthur	Kerrera	(03/11/1845)
Edward Hume	Kerrera	(06/06/1848)

On Kerrera James was noted for the production of quality cattle. Unfortunately after only seven years farming there, James, aged only 50 passed away on 1st May 1850, after catching a chill from being caught in a storm. His wife Jane took over with Duncan MacDougall as overseer.

Jane died at Ardentrive on 27th August 1856. The children carried on farming but eventually had to sell up after two years. They moved to Oban and went to live with their aunt and uncle, Isabella (nee Keddie) and Duncan MacArthur at Sorab House. The eldest daughter, Jane, died there aged only 23. The remaining family then decided to go to New Zealand and set sail on the 'Gala' under Captain Fisher on 18th November 1859, arriving at Port Chalmers in New Zealand on 22nd February 1860.

Catherine Ann Cameron, the eldest at 21 years old, wrote a letter, diary form, to her uncle and aunt, Duncan and Isabella MacArthur, whilst on board. At this point Edward the youngest was only 11 years old.

8th December 1859

My dearest Uncle & Aunt,

….I had to go to bed on Sabbath forenoon and did not re-appear till Tuesday afternoon. Johnie stayed till the Friday, the rest got on wonderfully. Many of the passengers are still far from well, even after three week's nautical experience. Just fancy, in the beginning of December we don't know what to do with the heat. We are within a week's sail of the line. Today we passed the Island of Antonia. Tell the children we are seeing immense shoals of flying fish, pretty little creatures.

We have never seen land since dear Scotland

faded from our view, on the memorable Saturday when we parted with dear Uncle. I never will forget the feeling of loneliness that came over me when the boat you were in went out of sight. But we are getting on pretty well. I am sometimes like to lose heart, for it is most miserable down below, but as long as we are on deck I was never in better spirits….

Everybody is feeling very far from being satisfied with the arrangements on board. The places down below are frightfully close and a shocking smell in this dreadful heat – it is quite suffocating. We get our things quite differently now, the whole of the people are divided into messes of nine, we get a week's allowance of tea, sugar, flour, oatmeal, biscuits, butter, suet, raisins, peppercorns, lime-juice, mustard and vinegar. We do have to exercise economy to make ends meet. The two young men who share the boys berth are included in our mess. The gardener one has turned out a most disagreeable fellow, he can't agree with anyone. When they were first in our mess they got a share of what was going every day but we soon found out we would have the worst of it, for instance the first week's supply of butter – we only had it to one meal. Jamie ate it all, biscuits we were a whole day short and just had to fast – but now on the days which the different provisions are served out, the boys measure out their share, so we are getting on a little better….

12th December 1859

…I can never feel thankful enough for your thoughtfulness, uncle dear, in giving me these oranges – ever since we left I have been taking one occasionally. When sick we suffer dreadfully from thirst and the water has been dreadfully bad, it has such a taste, now it is quite warm, when sick the smell of it was enough to overcome me. …If you ever come out be sure to bring a good supply of oranges and a water filter. They all get water filtered for the cabin and there is a very great difference. Another thing I am grateful we brought, is the disinfecting fluid, the people in the berth

next to us have a terrible smell. Oh! The most of them are a dirty set. I am afraid of disease breaking out amongst us….

17th December 1859

…Very hot below, but a pleasant breeze. Will cross the line tomorrow if spared. I never had any idea of what thirst was before. It is very calm – how different from the first week, such tossing and headings and noise of the sails and occasionally a flood of water coming down the hatchway was truly alarming to us land folks….

22 December 1859

Very close and hot. Have not been up on deck yet though it is five to one. Have been nursing Hugh – still very ill, but the fever accompanying is very much abated but very weak. I am thankful however he speaks quite coherently today.

21 January 1860

What a time has passed since I last wrote any of this letter. I have got out of the way of doing it now. Hugh and James were both laid up together and I can assure you I had enough to do. James got the better of his attack in a few days but Hugh was confined to bed for nearly a fortnight and even after getting up took a long time to come round, he got dreadfully thin, I never saw anyone so quickly reduced….

28 January 1860

….But when I begin to think of landing in Otago and no place to go to I do not weary so much….

30 January 1860

..I do weary for a quiet Sabbath again, there is little difference here from other days of the week…..

Looking out on the Ben Ohau plains.

22 February 1860

After two or three rough days we are now alongside Otago. A very rough looking place. Yet not more than our own rocky Scottish hills, they remind me much of Glencoe, but of course not so high. One of the hills we passed had the very shape and look of the Dunolly Hills, - they are all covered in brushwood....

The Cameron youngsters had a letter of introduction to the Rev. Dr Burns in Dunedin, who along with his wife settled them into a cottage. The boys started working immediately.

Seven years on, Hugh Cameron married Sarah Preston of Centrewood, Goodwood, Otago on 14/06/67 and took up Aviemore Station in North Otago. They had 12 children, five girls and seven boys: Elizabeth, Janie, James, Anne, Katie, Hugh, John (Jack), Joseph, Mary, Walter, Arthur and Fredrick.

Sarah Preston's brother, James Henry Preston married Margaret Ann Pringle in 1889 and purchased Ben Ohau Station in 1891.

Hugh and Sarah's son Jack alias J.E.P Cameron married Margaret Pringle, a 2nd cousin of James Preston's wife.

So it was James Preston's 21-year-old nephew Jack who became manager of Ben Ohau Station in 1897 and purchased it in 1901. Cameron descendants still own Aviemore and Otematata Stations as well Ben Ohau.

By 1911 the station had been reduced to some 64 000acres and Ben Ohau was split in four for soldier settlement 1920. The homestead block, which is still a Cameron stronghold was around 6500ha was further reduced by Hydro development to 5818ha. The other properties which were once part of the original Ben Ohau Station are: Ruataniwha (5700ha), Omahau and Bendrose (6100ha).

I opened and closed a rabbit-proof netted gate – evidence of the halcyon days of this dreaded pest which devoured and devastated acres of land in the High Country, before I drove through a couple of paddocks to get to the large shed to which I'd been directed. The rabbit was brought into the country by an Englishman, I my add.

Inside, I was welcomed by Simon and Priscilla Cameron, present day owners of Ben Ohau Station. With the help of some neighbours they were sorting Merino wethers into sizes. This was the beginning of a trial, which is practised in parts of Australia, housing Merinos indoors and protecting their wool and thus increasing the

value of the fleece covered with synthetic coats which are removed every six weeks for washing.

"Wool is my thing," said Simon, "we are experimenting with superfine wool production and have great expectations. The micron measures from 16-19m. Those we have housed have been selected on the finest and we are concentrating on producing clean, bright, white, attractive, stylish wool and still have a long way to go."

"The work been done to promote Merino wool has been tremendous and people are now getting to recognise superior wool. Merino NZ are concentrating on the top end of fashion with a lot of wool being exported to Italy and Germany."

"We have a small Merino stud and are mainly experimenting for our own commercial use," explains Simon.

After segregating the wethers into various lots according to live weights and size we adjourned to the farmhouse for afternoon tea, before Simon chauffeured me on a farm tour.

From a knoll behind the house we had a panoramic view of the property: one fifth was hilly, tussocky country, which has an average 90" rainfall compared to the meagre 19" on the plains.

"Around 500ha are developed and act as the 'engine room', fattening stock and producing hay for feeding out in winter", explained Simon.

For ease of management the Camerons purchase weaner steers to fatten rather than rearing their own, selling the Herefords and

Bunny proof fencing!

BEN OHAU STATION

Angus crosses as 2 year olds.

As well as the 2000 Merino ewes, 1200 wethers and 1100 retained lambs, Ben Ohau is home to 50 Angora goats. "We have been in the goat industry since 1978 and have stuck with them. They are easy care and are great weed control. The past couple of years have seen good dividends for quality mohair."

We returned to the homestead and were greeted by the two beautiful young blonde Cameron daughters: Janie (11) and Sarah (9), who had just come home from school. I was kindly invited to join them all for the evening meal and to view a video of Ben Ohau on a Gaelic programme – 'Eilean Eile'. It was strange hearing my mother tongue so far from home.

The Camerons' in-house sheep venture was a tremendous success as they achieved a 104kg bale of ultra fine wool fine merino wool (13.2 micron) selling through agents Pyne Gould Guinness at the Christchurch Wool Sale for $528 a kilogram greasy.

The New Zealand record stands at $1200 a kg for 13.1 micron from veteran grower Donald Burnett, Mt Cook Station, in 1999. The Cameron's sold their bale just two days after the terrorist attacks in America on September 11th when prices had plummeted.

Ben Ohau will be on the map once more – this time on the Big Screen Blockbuster – Lord of the Rings. Extensive filming for part three of the trilogy saw over 800 people and numerous horses descend onto this High Country property. (Yours truly was incidentally an extra – playing the part of a refugee in the scenes at Deer Park Heights with the awesome Remarkables in the background.)

Goats on Ben Ohau.

Priscilla Cameron and one of the housed, superfine wethers.

BEN OMAR STATION

'The glorious twelfth,' noted worldwide as the commencement of the Scottish Grouse shooting season, was upon us once more. New Zealand, a great sporting nation, which devotes about 30 minutes of the National news each evening to sport, has its own version – duck shooting. May 1st each year marks opening day for duck shooting, a date which is rated highly on the sporting and social calendar. The season lasts until the last Saturday in July.

Here in New Zealand one does not have to be blessed with a doubled barrelled surname, wear tweeds and plus fours and speak with a plum in ones mouth – it is a sport for one and all and certainly doesn't cost $1000 a pop. Most farming properties boast a duck pond and some serious duck shooters feed the ducks for weeks in advance to ensure plenty will be about on opening day.

I was lucky enough to be invited along for opening day by 'Ginger' Anderson – New Zealand's' top sheep dog trialist. With invites to the fairer sex few and far between, I jumped at the opportunity.

Lindsay Purvis, an ex deer farmer now in the tourist industry – selling souvenirs and afternoon teas to Japanese bus parties, master of the Mai-mai, (hide) was worried in case I'd turn up in pink or some other bright colour and frighten off the birds. PINK!!! – I have not worn any shade of pink since the Agric Ball on my third year at Edinburgh. Us girlies had wintered rather well (real heifers!!) and our live weight gain would have delighted any finishing farmer.

Back to the matter in hand; rising at some unearthly hour, about 5am, I made my way into Omarama, suitably dressed in dark clothes and a Driza-bone, to the local pub for the compulsory duck shooting breakfast. In the packed dining room the male: female ratio was rather pleasing, with two of us ladies to about fifty blokes – the other girl being the waitress! I joined Ginger, Lindsay and Dalrachney Station owner Rick Aubrey at the table but opted for tea and toast rather than a greasy fry up.

The Kiwis were decked out mainly in camouflage gear and after a hearty breakie we headed out in our wee groups to the maimais before daylight. Our hut was a bit more elaborate than I had expected – we had comfortable armchairs, a heater, BBQ, and a shooting deck, camouflaged with tussocks and plastic army foliage – all we needed was mud on our faces to look the part!

We sat conversing in whispers in the darkness waiting for daylight to break. Lindsay decided to put the competition at a disadvantage by ringing local publican, Peter Casserly on his cell phone and frightening the ducks from their pond before dawn! We all thought this a great joke as we sipped our early morning port.

Around 7am the volleys of fire could be heard from neighbouring duck ponds and our crew took up some serious shooting.

My previous encounters with firearms were limited: clay pigeon shooting with a friend and out at night on the hill with neighbouring farmers – John MacDairmid and Iain Morrison aka

Reflections at duckshooting.

Mochann after a fox on my lambing beat at home on Skye. In the former instance I had beginners luck and hit the first four out of five shells and the latter – needless to say I wasn't allowed near the gun!

Eventually I was offered a shot at the ducks and the guys seemed to find it very amusing that I'd line up for a shot and as I pulled the trigger I'd look away to avoid getting so much recoil. But my technique seemed to work to a certain degree and I managed to shoot a couple.

By lunchtime we had an entourage of visitors in the hut, from other mai-mais and some locals who were just cruising round socialising. The Kiwis certainly know how to eat heartily and the usual New Zealand country fare was on offer: duck, oysters, venison and lamb.

Around three o'clock we all adjourned to the local pub, owned by ex-blade shearer and current blade record holder– Peter Casserly – shearing 353 lambs in 8 hours in 1976 at Mt Somers. There we laid out our ducks in competition with the other shooters and I'm proud to say that our contingent won hands down. I was also awarded the 'best looking duck shooter', but as the only female it was a bit of a breeze!

Lindsay Purvis, Eilidh MacPherson and Ginger Anderson pose in the mai mai.   *Going for a duck!* *Duck wing.*   *The team*   *Duck plucking*

Duck shooters at the Omarama Pub.

Autumnal colours. Decoy ducks float in the foreground near the Mai mai on the left.

Before dusk we headed off for another round at the hide. Things began to liven up and by the end of the evening we had a rare old ceilidh going in the hut.

The following day we all met up in Omarama for duck plucking. They were dipped in a vat of hot wax enabling the feathers to be pulled off much more easily.

No newcomer to the dog trialling game Ginger ran his first dog Ben in 1965 and won the local North Otago trial. From then on it has been a steady stream of winning tickets, trophies and titles, locally, nationally and internationally for this acclaimed Ben Omar Station owner. His CV includes 9 Island Championships, two New Zealand Titles, 13 NZ finals and a TV trial competition. He has also represented NZ six times, captaining it for 4 of these, judged in NZ, Australia and America and run dogs in 46 national run-offs.

Ginger attributes his great line of working and trialling dogs to his ancestors who ran the Ardlui pub on the shores of Loch Lomond and brought their collie dogs with them when they came out to New Zealand.

John Anderson (his great grandfather) came out from Ardlui and became head shepherd on Benmore Station, Omarama on 29 August 1899.

Open day on Ben Omar   *John and Ginger Anderson*

Jim Murray and his team of dogs take off on the straggle muster on Glenmore Station

GLENMORE STATION

Since my first visit to New Zealand back in 1991, I have found Lake Tekapo enchanting, almost spiritual. So visiting a high country station on the shores of this awe-inspiring lake was more than just an ordinary interview and adventure for me.

Jim Murray, current laird of Glenmore, (third generation) whose family have been running the property since 1918 kindly invited me to join him on his autumn cattle muster. We headed out from the homestead in a 4WD Toyota Hilux, the best selling all terrain vehicles in New Zealand, laden with dogs, cut lunches and hill sticks.

The 19 500 ha holding has two main valleys: the Forks and the Cass with access up the river beds, so we were in for a bumpy ride. The scenery was indescribable – just breath taking with snow capped peaks looming to 7500 feet, part of the Leibig Range.

Our mission was to take sixty Angus cattle from the Forks to lower ground for the winter, for calving and more shelter from the elements. The Murrays run 250 Angus breeding cows, 360

total, including followers. "It is a weaner operation," explained Mr Murray, " all calves are sold in Temuka mid April."

Driving along the flood plains we passed black cattle grazing but we carried on, stopping for a look at the backcountry hut, which stands, at an altitude of just over 3000 feet. We left the truck there and Jim and I carried on walking up the riverbed while the single shepherd tackled the right hand-side face and ridge.

Jim has run the property from 1965/66 and then bought it his fathers' estate in 1968. At that point there were 5500 sheep and 80 cattle. Nowadays he is running 10 000 merinos, mainly ewes, 800 deer and the aforementioned suckler cows totalling 14 000 stock units.

"We breed our own rams and sell some privately locally. We aim for 19 micron and sell wool on contract to Ice Breaker."

Every so often the tall, wiry high country run holder would stop and scan the steep faces for any stragglers left behind from the autumn muster. He was a man of few words, but when

he did speak it was worth waiting for and some dry humour would sneak out every now and again. After some time Jim spied a few Merino wethers through his binoculars and made off with his canine entourage up the face which backs onto Braemar Station on the shores of Lake Pukaki. The station is also bounded by Godley Peaks Station to the north, the Ministry of Defence (Mount John) to the south and the shores of Lake Tekapo on the east. I tootled on up the riverbed, taking pictures, enjoying the wilderness and watching Jim's progress as I went.

There were fourteen escape artists in the mob and they were not keen to come down at all – they stood their ground and foot-stomped at the dogs before co-operating. Hard to say how high up they were but a good 1500 feet at a guess, so it took a fair time to coax and hunt them off their patch.

"They are stragglers from Braemar," Jim informed me when the expedition had reached the valley floor and we were reunited. We retraced our steps following the 'wrinklies' along

the rough, boulder and shingle strewn, dry, river flood plain. The river crossing proved another hurdle with the fully woollen clad ovines very reluctant to take the icy plunge.

Back at the hut I was promoted to truck driver and did my best to keep to a track, as I rocked and rolled all the way back. The musterer had just pushed the cattle through the gate and helped us corner the sheep behind it and manhandle them into the back of the ute.

The first shepherds on Glenmore Station found primitive sheep yards and it was suspected that Mackenzie the sheep stealer had built and used them. Apparently a stray sheep was also found near Glenmore, between Lake Pukaki and Lake Tekapo in1856. The finder – John McHutcheson, the first Mackenzie Country settler reckoned it must have been a straggler from Mackenzie's first mob. "..it was in fine condition and had a grand fleece of wool some 16in to 18in in length," wrote McHutcheson.

John McGregor, who had shepherded on the Grampians Station, secured a licence for a tract of land in the forks of the Cass River in 1873 and named it Glenmore. He realised this country was too cold for wintering sheep so two years on he had secured neighbouring Castle Hall station in partnership with Tom Macdonald and John and William Robinson and ran both as Glenmore.

Castle Hall Station was initially known as Gristhope, named by Joseph Beswick who took up the 8000ha property in 1858. He was friendly with and worked for the Hall brothers who had Mount Hutt and Springfield stations in Mid Canterbury and Balmoral and the Mistake in Mackenzie. Due to financial difficulties and low wool prices Beswick sold out to John Hall in 1867 and the name subsequently changed to Castle Hall.

John Hall went into politics, being first chair of Christchurch Town Council, elected to the House of Representatives and in 1879 became Premier of New Zealand. His most remarkable achievement was having his Female Franchise Bill (the right for women to vote) passed and become law in 1893. He sold Castle Hall to Alfred Cox in 1872.

John McGregor was born in Banffshire, Scotland and came out to New Zealand in 1860. He along with Harry

Run 79 – the Murrays shop in Tekapo.

Over ewe go!!

Ford had driven one of the first flocks from North Canterbury into the Mackenzie country in May that same year. They were on foot for the whole journey and spent two days waist high in water swimming the flock across the flooded Rakaia. Apparently they were nearly swept off their feet on several occasions "but we got those sheep to the Grampians without losing a hoof," regaled McGregor.

In 1878 this canny Scotsman was elected onto the Mount Cook Road Board and served on it for 21 years. When the district became a county in 1883 and the Mackenzie County Council was formed – John McGregor was the first chairman.

Homeward bound along a dry river bed.

Following the real hard winter of 1888, when sheep losses were incurred on Glenmore, McGregor left the station in 1891, when the New Zealand Loan and Mercantile Agency Company took it over for the next twenty years.

A couple of owners: Miss Roma Hope and then Herbert Nadar had Glenmore short term from 1912. On the latter's death the property was passed on to Mrs Mary Murray in 1918, whose son Gerald ran the property (grand father of the present day owner). The Murray family originated from Blair Athol, Scotland.

It was coming on dusk by the time we pulled into the yard; having pushed the cattle another

Musterers hut on Glenmore.

few kilometres down a track to their new winter grazing. The Murrays, in time honoured high country fashion offered me an evening meal, but the lure of a Scottish Ceilidh dance in Wanaka was too much for this Scot.

Since my visit to Glenmore Station, Jim and Anne Murray have diversified and made use of their location by opened a clothing outlet in Tekapo – RUN 79 – offering an array of labelled merino woollens to satisfy any discerning tourist or native. Original works by local artists, including some by Anne Murray herself, are also on offer.

Merinos and dogs

NOKOMAI STATION

I first met the Nokomai head shepherd – Daniel Price – at the Coronet Peak Ski Field Dog Derby, near Queenstown, where as winner of the event I interviewed him for the New Zealand Farmer. Later at the Bark Up at Arthur's' Point Pub, when I explained to him that I was researching for a book on the Stations established by Scotsmen, he insisted that Nokomai must be included in my travels.

A Bark Up is another entertaining Kiwi pub competition, where the shepherds allow their dogs to flaunt their canine vocal chords. One by one the four-legged competitors take to the podium – usually some bales of straw – and on command, howl and yap to their hearts content. A panel of judges award points for the rowdiest performance.

Some months later, having read a bit more of the history of the station, which was taken up in 1859 by Donald Cameron, I contacted Daniel and went to join the tailing (lamb marking) gang for a few days work in the yards, mustering and the chance for some awesome photo shots.

During my visit, the work force for tailing consisted of three full time shepherds; Matt Black, Chris Anderson and Jason Woodham, head stockman Daniel Price, 2 casual shepherds; Cameron Scott (Taraunga), Danny Hayes (Otautau) and James Hore (26), the present owners' son.

The boys were great craic to work with and didn't seem to mind a Scottish intruder. They all seemed rather keen to get their picture in print and were positively delighted when I said I'd give them all a mention in the Acknowledgements.

Tailing was ultra organised as such huge numbers of lambs had to be dealt with as quickly as possible. Two conveyor type chutes were used to restrict the lamb's movement while teams of shepherds worked swiftly: castrating (using rubber rings), tailing (with a burner, which seals the laceration) and ear marking.

Later, Daniel drove Matt, Chris, Cameron, with a team about five dogs apiece, and me, up a narrow winding ledge to the summit of the block where the view with the snow-capped

Remarkable and Richardson Mountains in the distance was breathtaking.

Rising from 250m at the homestead, to 1889m along the top of the Garvie Mountains, this impressive holding shares a 50km boundary fence with the well-known Glenaray Station, run by David Pickney. Glenaray is only one of fifteen properties, neighbouring Nokomai, many of the others also brandish Scottish place names: Lorne Peak, Loch Linnie, Glen Nevis, Ben Nevis, Carrick, Earnscleugh and Glenlapa Stations to name but a few. The shepherds knowledgeably pointed out landmarks and the direction of the other stations if they were not visible.

The original name 'Glenfalloch', used by Donald Cameron, the Scottish Highlander who first laid claim to Run 354, the now Nokomai Station, in early 1859, describes this property to a 'T'. Coming from his (and my) mother tongue – Scottish Gaelic – the word 'falach' translates to 'hidden' in the English language.

This picturesque, secluded valley is situated, seemingly in a world of it's own, only 12km

Shepherds; Matt Black, Chris Anderson and Cameron Scott and their dogs heading off to muster a block on Nokomai

Winners of the Dog Derby, Daniel Price and Wag

Cameron Scott's dogs: York, Sam and Prem, 'bark up' on command.

down a gravel road off State Highway 6, just south of the village of Athol in Northern Southland.

Donald Angus Cameron, a carpenters' son, born to Ewen and Catherine (née McPhee), on 8 August 1835 at Fort William, by the foot of Ben Nevis, Scotland, the eldest of six, attended high school at Fort William before heading to Glasgow aged 14 as a shipping clerk. His ancestors were the Camerons of Glen Nevis and the Camerons of Letterfinlay. He set out for South Australia to work for his great-uncle, Alexander Cameron, at Limestone Ridge Station, Penola in 1854, when he was 19.

By 1858 Donald was managing Mt Sturgeon Plains Station and decided to take up land in New Zealand early the following year. With a relation, Angus MacDonald, the two pioneers set out, accompanied by a Maori known as 'Sandfly', to explore the unsurveyed eastern side of Lake Wakatipu. Apparently they were the first to scale the sheer promontory they came across which they named, 'the Devil's Staircase'. That treacherous part of Highway 6 still bears the name to this day. Other mountains and rivers they named after places in their homeland include; the Locky, Roy and Nevis Rivers, Ben Nevis, Lorne Peak and the Lumber Box. These hardy Scots returned to Dunedin where DA Cameron staked a claim on Run 331 (Staircase) before they returned to Australia for stock.

By June 1859 the first 1500 sheep arrived at Bluff aboard the Peregrine Oliver but tragedy struck as the sheep had been dipped prior to their voyage in a mixture of tobacco, arsenic, sulphur and soda and 2333 out of the total 3592 were asphyxiated and pushed to a watery grave. Of the remainder another 452 were lost on the gruelling overland journey from Bluff, leaving only 807. Due to these losses, the Staircase Run was relinquished, so Donald applied for neighbouring Run 354 – Nokomai – which he acquired in March 1860. That same year, he built the first dwelling, woolshed and yards following a dire winter camped in the snow.

Gold was first discovered in the Nokomai Valley in 1862 and the population boomed to 1000 within a couple of years. The station provided meat and potatoes for the gold diggers.

Donald, a devout Catholic and proud Scotsman, married Margaret MacDonald at St Patrick's Cathedral in Melbourne, before taking his new bride home to Glenfalloch. The couple had 7 children: 5 daughters and two sons. Ewen Cameron, Donald's father made the trip out to join the family once his wife Catherine had passed away in the late 1860's.

By 1870 there were 8000 sheep on Nokomai and over the following two decades numbers had increased to 13 000. Not only was Cameron increasing his stocking rates but he was also increasing his land holdings: Closeburn Station on Lake Wakatipu, Fassifern near Tapanui, and further properties at Mabel Bush and Mataura.

Donald Cameron, a native Gaelic speaker, piper and first Chief of the

Lake Wakatipu and the Devil's Staircase.

Highland Society of Southland, occupied the property for 6 decades (which in 1936 was a record for Otago and Southland and probably still is) until his death on Nokomai on Hogmanay 1918. It remained, as a trust, in the Cameron family until Frank Hore purchased it in 1950. Frank still resides on the station, but handed the reins over to his son Brian in 1985, following on from a father/son partnership, which was established in 1960.

After three days tailing and mustering with the permanent staff and casual musterers, in awesome weather and surroundings followed by a works night out in Mossburn joined by boss' daughter, Chrissie Hore, I finally managed to pin the busy owner, Brian Hore, down to an interview early one morning.

Presently the Nokomai Run covers some 38000ha including the 1200ha Parawa Downs, which was purchased 27 years back and Flagstaff Station (2290ha) which came into the fold more recently – only a decade ago.

"To a large extent they are run as one, our strength being that they all link up geographically. Mark Thomas and Grey Stewart manage Parawa Downs and Flagstaff respectively," said Brian.

The Hores are presently in the process of converting their 15,000 strong wether contingent from Half breds to Merinos, in a bid to increase the value of the wool clip. Over the past couple of years around 3000 Half bred wether lambs have been wintered and exchanged for Merino hoggets in the spring. This conversion is about the half way mark now.

Half bred cross Romney ewes, numbering 27 000, are the base flock grazing the Garvie and Hector Mountain ranges of this high country station. The lion's share (just under 16 000 ewes), run with Halfbred rams, which are bred 'in-house', so to speak, at Parawa.

Parawa Station located on the main drag, at the turn-off to Nokomai, acts as the breeding and recording nucleus for both sheep and cattle enterprises on the property. Not only are stud

Halfbreds produced there, but it is also home to Romney, Texel, Merino and Hereford studs. Brian's wife and business partner, Ann, is responsible for the input and update of all recording data for both sheep and cattle studs.

Romney rams cover another 4000 ewes and the older ewes, 6000 in total, are mated with a terminal sire. Texel is the preferred breed and has been used by the Hores' since its' inception to New Zealand in 1991 when Nokomai was involved in a group-breeding scheme along with the Aitkens of Glenayr and Mt Linton Station. Over the nine-year period, stud ewe numbers have been built up to 200 from the initial 11. "We have just sent some Texel rams to the Falkland Islands," adds Ann, "good feet were their most important criterion due to the long distances they had to cover on the islands. They also choose a southern based stud so the rams will be more acclimatised to the conditions on the Falkland Islands."

Some big changes have taken place over the

past few years by using terminal sires over a higher proportion of the flock, paying more attention to objective measurement and the selection of rams hence producing the kind of meat lamb that is demanded by the export market. "The biggest barrier is that the Texel is treated as any other carcase. The Texel Society should be looking at a niche marketing initiative, but supply must be guaranteed."

During tailing it was easy to spot the Texel cross lambs - they had excellent conformation with uniform width from hip to shoulder and good body depth. This factor ensures that the chop eye muscle is consistent the length of the carcass. Well-developed hindquarters, with a full gigot, spelling out a 'U' rather than a 'V' between the legs also differentiated the breeds. This is very much what the UK and European markets require.

Since the introduction of fresh, chilled lamb overseas, the meat industries both here and abroad are demanding uniform lamb carcases of a

A well earned break for man and dogs.

The guys stop to pose for a picture.

higher calibre. A new grading system is in the offing to identify superior meat carcases and pay accordingly.

Carcases should be more compact than rangy and leggy, like a lot of traditional wool or dual-purpose breeds. The chump should be well muscled, the middle long and fore quarter lean.

The Alliance Group (where all Nokomai Texel progeny are hung up, averaging 16kgs) are moving with the times and intend to install 3D imagery to make grading objective rather than subjective. They aim to reward for quality, with well muscled, good yielding carcases receiving considerably more than long leg, poor conformation, low yielding counterparts.

The 'Continentals' as they are referred to in the United Kingdom, or 'Exotics' over here, used as Terminal Sires over the native breeds or as pure breds, seem to satisfy market requirements. The Texel has undoubtedly come out trumps, with the Beltex, Charolais, Rouge de le Quest, Blue du Maine and a range of others having all made an appearance and having varying degrees of success in the UK as more recently the Dorper imported from South Africa has over here.

Annually 200 000kgs of wool is trucked off the station, "I'm very supportive of the McKinsey Report and it is pleasing to see parties coming together as it looked like Strong wools were going to become fragmented," said Brian who has been involved with the mid-micron group. " We have been let down by wools of New Zealand in the last few years and by spreading options and niche marketing we may look forward to a brighter future."

"Lice and fly control is a problem, but we have found an electric eye dip, which cuts out when no sheep are in it, to be successful on the lambs. There is a fine line between dipping fine wool and controlling lice so no residues are detectable in the fleece at shearing. WoolPro are working on this problem as we speak."

The latest project that has been undertaken by the Hores' is to introduce a new type of Merino

L to r– Matt Black, Kit Fox, Cameron Scott, Chris Anderson and Jason Woodhouse.

to the existing Polled Merino Stud on their 354ha Corbridge Downs property at Wanaka. These Merinos have a Soft Rolling Skin, little wrinkle and grow soft fine wool.

One hundred ewes close to SRS type were artificially inseminated. "The idea is to try SRS over our existing Halfbred ewes," he said. Thirty ewes have had embryos transplanted.

The 950 strong Hereford suckler herd is now almost a closed operation as all replacement bulls used are bred at the Hereford Stud on Flagstaff Station. Around a dozen extra commercial sires are sold off the property. Potential sires are selected on performance and confirmation as well as recorded birth weights and liveweight gain through to 600kgs.

The cattle were originally of Braxton lineage and until recently there was an ongoing AI programme using American semen. The cattle

usually scan on 95% and any dry cows are culled.

For the past five years the policy at Nokomai has been to carry all the calves through to two year olds and sell them as forward stores on the property. Agents, Wrightsons sell the Herefords on a per kg live weight basis.

"We are entirely reliant on good staff and some that will take responsibility. Over the past few years, there has been a shortage of staff for stock work in the high country, but those that are available are extremely willing and keen," enthused Brian.

"I'm personally not in favour of tenure review in the High Country. Free-holding is beneficial as otherwise large tracts of land, which are required in the summer and are vital for the balance of a property, can be lost."

The Hores freeholded one lease at Fiery Creek, south of the Mataura River, through the

voluntary tenure review process. "It is not really a loss – I saw it more of a liability as Wilding trees (Pinus Contorta), which could be the scourge of tussock land, if not controlled, were spreading from Mid Dome."

"Generally speaking, I'm not sure DOC have the ability to look after all these high country places, but I give them credit for the control of Pinus Contorta at Fiery Creek."

Brian, who is presently the Chairman of the Southland High Country Section of Federated Farmers, thinks that run-holders have lost a lot of ground with the restrictions on what they are allowed to do with land environmentally under the new Pastoral Land Bill.

Nokomai is also one of the satellite farms involved with the Hill Country Tussock Development Group. "The group has done some trial work following what has been carried out at

Action on Nokomai with tailing in full swing using portable yards.

Parawa and Mount Linton, investigating ways of introducing new grasses and clovers to give better performance on high country as well as lime trials."

The biggest output on this high country station is fertiliser as 10,000ha are doctored on a rotational basis. Last season 1150t of Sulphurised Super were flown on and 150t applied by spreader as well as 400t of lime.

Other farm related groups Mr Hore is involved in include the Texel Society and Chair of Phoenix Aviation topdressing company.

Nokomai now offers the discerning tourist 'an Exquisite New Zealand Holiday Experience.' Accommodation is available in three luxury cottages on the station. Guests can relax and explore the isolation of the Hidden Valley by walking or mountain biking on some of the tracks, fishing on the Mataura River or watching farm activities.

Since his return home, James Hore, a professional pilot, has established Nokomai Helicopters. When he is not busy mustering stock on farm he offers guests a range of excursions: heli-fishing, heli-touring, heli-hiking, heil-hunting, heli-biking or a champagne flight in a Bell Jet Ranger, a Cessna 206 plane or a DH82A Tiger Moth Bi-plane.

In the winter months tourists can even take guided tours through the Garvie Mountains on snowmobiles.

On the top beat with Cameron Scott.   *Birds eye view of the hidden valley.*

Johnny Templeton, manager of Walter Peak Station meets us at the TTS Earnslaw, Lake Wakatipu.

WALTER PEAK
STATION

The mention of Walter Peak Station conjures up images of hoards of tourists aboard the T.T.S. Earnslaw, having afternoon tea and singing songs with a piano accompanist, heading across Lake Wakatipu for their New Zealand 'station experience' – a sheep shearing demonstration and a few Highland cows.

In reality, only 167 hectares of Walter Peak Station, including the original homestead, on the shores of Lake Wakatipu were sold off in 1968 for the tourism venture. The present homestead and station buildings were relocated some four kilometres inland.

My first trip to Walter Peak was on a bleak August day in miserable weather conditions. A Pommy friend – Priscilla – and I took the Steamer the TTS Earnslaw over the lake and were met by the station manager in a Toyota Hilux on the slipway on the other side. He gave us a quick tour of the terraced flats as the high ground was completely obliterated by a drizzly mist and took us back to the homestead to warm up with cups of tea while we chatted.

With 26 700 hectares carrying 20 000 stock units at his disposal, manager John Templeton, has set rigorous targets for himself to achieve over the next few years. He aims to increase production levels by at least 10% and stocking rates by 5000 units.

Over the past six years no Super has been applied to the property and John enthusiastically sees "endless potential in the place." He has been applying 400t of Super Phosphate: 250t aerially and 150t by bulk which will inevitably increase the feed available and enable a direct proportional increase in stock numbers.

The 10 000 Merinos had been producing a lambing percentage between 85 and 90% and wool weights of an average 3.8 kilos. "I would like to see 100% lambing and wool production rising to 4.5kgs," said John.

"At the moment the ewe wool measures up at 20.2m which I would like to lower to 19.2micron as there is no premium above that figure. The hoggets average 18.2 and the wethers 19 micron."

The vital spark in rectifying and fine-tuning the quality of the woolclip at Walter Peak has been activated by the introduction of finer fleeced sires from Bob Brown, Glenthorne and Bill and Andrew Sutherland of Benmore Station.

All the ewes were machine-shorn pre-lamb with cover combs from 28 August and the hoggets and wethers lose their winter coats in the middle of October courtesy of Andrew Clegg's gang. "Blade shearing is too slow and expensive," he said.

The scanning figures, monitored by Brent Burges, were on the up at 111% for the pure Merinos and 121% for the Cull Merinos, which were mated with a Perendale ram. Merino two-tooths, 600 in total, are 59% in lamb and 37% of 180 hoggets are carrying a lamb. "Our policy is to put every hogget weighting over 40kgs to a ram."

The main health problems encountered, with running the Merinos on a relatively high rainfall property are as expected: foot rot and wool rot. Zinc Sulphate is applied via a walk through shower after shearing to prevent the latter.

"I intend to increase the 1100 strong Perendale flock to 2500 ewes. They have been preforming at 130% lambing and I'm aiming for 140%. This year they scanned at 160% so it is looking promising. The 400 Merino Texel crosses do not yield much wool and the fertility is not great, but they are vigorous fern grazers," commented John.

All ewes are lambed on the 1052ha of over-sown country and remain there until weaning at the end of January. The ewes then go onto the summer country until the middle of April when they are taken into mid altitude paddocks, covering some 3000ha for tupping.

"The 5000 Merino wethers are put out on the back boundary – Whiteburn and Blackspurs in early May until the beginning of October pre shearing. There is a snow fence above them at 3000 feet. After shearing the wethers tidy up the fern on the front hill blocks until Christmas."

Hoggets and lambs are pampered on the front paddocks, with all lambs

being grass finished. "Last season we fattened the lambs and hung them up at 15.2kgs dead weight with Alliance at their Omarau plant and hope to do likewise this year."

Presently there are 600 Hereford cattle grazing the slopes of Walter Peak, " I want to run 400 Hereford/ Angus cross cows and cover them with a Shorthorn bull, keeping 200 Herefords as a base for replacements. I feel the Shorthorn, which is not so stocky – rangier – is making a come back. Richard Kerr from Wendonside, near Waikaka has top class Shorthorn sires and we source our Angus sires from Stern at Kakahu."

John and wife Sharon returned to the Wakatipu area in November 1998 where they had met 13 years previously. Sharon had been working on the Walter Peak tourist enterprise and John had been shepherding on neighbouring Mt Nicholas. Following eight years of shepherding in both North and South Islands, including stints on: Benmore, Ben Omar and Lake

Hay time, Walter Peak

Looking over to Walter Peak

Ohau, John managed Mararoa Station and Burwood before taking on this challenging high country position at Walter Peak. Farming must be in the genes as his father and grandfather before him were both managers: the former with Landcorp at Te Anau and the latter at Makarora, Wanaka.

Since his arrival at Walter Peak, John has been too preoccupied, on station, to follow his favourite pastime - the dog trials, but he hopes to do so this coming season. He has qualified for numerous National Trials in both heading and huntaway classes over the years and a 2nd in the Zig Zag Hunt with 'Trode', in 1998, is his highest accolade to date.

Sharon, a city chick, who has adapted well to high country life, tends to the farm accounts, cooks for the two single shepherds and also for the four casuals at mustering time, as well as caring for the couple's one-year old daughter. With a young child in tow Sharon finds she now has less spare time for her horses.

Weather for ducks!

More and more overseas investors seem to be snapping up land in New Zealand and Walter Peak is no exception with International owners: Ian Koblick, of Florida, one of the joint run holders of Walter Peak, is a Marine Biologist and comes to the station for three-month stints now and again. The Khans, Morris and Ben, on the other hand are more like sleeping partners. Of Israeli origin, they now abide in South Africa.

Stepping back in time, in the Wakatipu area, when white man arrived, some Maori activity was noted in the form of camp ovens and greenstone implements, but none of the early pioneers mentioned having actually come across any Maori people in their diaries or memoirs.

Nathaniel Chalmers, who was born in Rothesay, Scotland, arrived in Invercargill in July 1853 and was the first white man to see the lake while travelling with Maori guides – Reko and Kaikoura. He was also the first Pakeha to canoe down the Shotover River (initially named the

All baled up.

Hamish Macdonald ensures a safe crossing.

WALTER PEAK STATION

Tummel by Robert Cameron) – which many tourists pay for the privilege nowadays.

But it was Donald Hay from Adelaide in Australia – probably an exiled Scot himself or with Scottish parentage – who was undoubtedly the first man to set foot on the present homestead area of Walter Peak. Accompanied by Donald Cameron of Glenfalloch Station (the now Nokomai), he climbed the Hector Mountains in July 1859 and Cameron showed him Lake Wakatipu for the first time. Hay was inspired with the vista below and returned a couple of months later, riding to Kingston at the end of the Lake with Cameron. He decided that the best way to explore the area would be by raft (as the lake is some 52 miles long and seven miles wide at the broadest part).

Setting out from Kingston on his solo voyage on a raft made of flax, as Donald Cameron was unable to join him, he spent the next two weeks exploring the vicinity in the cold of the August 1859 winter. He stopped off at Halfway Bay, Kawarau, Beach Bay, and the mouth of what has since named the Von River, Queenstown Bay and Bob's Cove. He also explored extensively on foot and Lake Hayes near Arrowtown bears his name, as does an annual boat race, still run, from Queenstown to Kingston and back.

Hay then returned to Kingston and rested up for a few days on Glenquoich (hollow in the hill) Station at Athol – home of William Cameron, brother of Donald. At the time, Robert and Archie Cameron were managing the property. He then made off to Dunedin to apply for the Walter Peak country, which he had explored only to be forestalled by a speculator. He was so disgusted he left New Zealand and did not return. On the roadside from Queenstown to Kingston sits a huge glacial rock with two black marble plaques mounted on it. On closer inspection one of these tablets displays Donald Hays' name and the other is in memory of Donald A Cameron of Glenfalloch and his friend Alex MacDonald of Reaby.

"....beyond the high ranges there's land for the men that first track their way through....
Sheep country in plenty....
I looked at the ranges, the white snow ranges, all faint in the sunshine and backed by the blue;
No white man had crossed them....
All day we rode onward – slow work on the boulders, and rough on the horses and worse on the men:
We lay in the lee of a rock that had fallen far down from a cliff that ran up out of sight;
It was colder than winter....
Then we reached the safe level, the bush and tussocks, the broad rolling slopes where our flocks would be fed;
There's smiling sheep country beyond the white ranges..."

David McKee Wright from "The Station Ballads"

Sunset over Lake Wakatipu.

Hamish Macdonald and Matt Stalker look on with their dogs.

Scotsman - Hugh MacKenzie, successfully established Walter Peak as a sheep station. It had been farmed previously but had been abandoned as it was over run with rabbits.

Hugh Mackenzie (b 19/10/1847) was the seventh child of crofters John and Ann Mackenzie of Ardmore in Sutherland. Hugh joined the Navy on leaving school and became a chief gunner on the Iron Duke before he had to retire due to ill health. He came out to New Zealand with his new bride – Anastasia McKenzie Rossiter in 1874 on the Cathcart.

Hugh then joined his brother Alexander in partnership on Coronet Peak Station. The winter of 1878 was extremely harsh and these two hardy pioneers, who were used to adverse weather conditions, coming from the far North of Scotland, spent 22 days snow-raking to save their 6000 strong flock. They sheared 5000 sheep that year, while many of their neighbours suffered severe losses. Due to these conditions and low wool prices, the brothers decided to sell Coronet

Peak and took up a 450acre farm at Walter Peak instead. They mustered, rabbited and fished to supplement their income. Five years on, the pair went their own ways: Alexander took up land at the head of Lake Wakatipu and the Waste Lands Board granted Hugh 10000 acres on Walter Peak.

A man of great determination and character, along with his family of six sons: John, Alex, Hugh, Peter, William and Walter and two daughters: Margaret and Anastasia, he set to and reduced the rabbit population, lifted stones, ploughed and sowed the lakeside terraces, erected sheep yards, housing, outhouses and fencing without borrowing any money.

MacKenzie set his children to work at an early age and John, the eldest, was taking a beat on the hills well before he hit his teens. This stood him in good stead as he later was in charge of all hill work on Walter Peak. Boundary keeping was a favourite job of the fit young lads as some of the terrain was so, that fencing was impractical and natural boundaries were used as they still are in

many cases today.

As the family grew up Hugh decided it was time to expand and in 1902 John and Alex moved to the upper Nevis run, but they held this for just two years as they found it was only suitable to graze wethers. They then took over Wyuna, at the head of Lake Wakatipu, from their Uncle Alex, as he was an aging bachelor.

By 1904 Hugh, extended his pastoral empire further by buying the neighbouring runs of Mt Nicholas and Fernhill and running them as Walter Peak Station, covering some 178 000 acres of crown land plus some more as freehold. John and Alex returned home and passed on the management of Wyuna to a cousin – Peter MacKenzie. Five of the MacKenzie sons and the two daughters joined their father to form a syndicate to farm the MacKenzie kingdom profitably. The sheep numbers rose, over the next fifty odd years, from 300 in 1882 to 40 000 by 1933.

In the winter of 1906, one of the MacKenzie

boys – William (21) headed out against his father's wishes to hunt the dark faces under the far side of Walter Peak itself. But on his return journey he met with a snow slide and tumbled to his death a couple of hundred feet below. A marble head stone marks the place where William met his end. Another son, Walter, was later killed in action at Gallipoli in 1915. Peter who rose to the position of Colonel, was badly gassed but made it home and took over the administration on the station.

The MacKenzies were the first to erect hill-country fences, much to the disdain of their neighbours, but they found that it reduced hogget loses and proved that fences could stand in snow country if the wires were kept tight. They erected over 150 miles of fencing over a 17-year period on the station. These fit young men also became excellent boatmen as the only access to the station was via the Lake and the family were renowned for rowing the 18 miles across the Lake to Queenstown and back to attend church.

The Clan MacKenzie scoured their own wool and visitors to the station would see masses of white fleeces lying in the paddocks during part of the scouring process. Topping the London sales for New Zealand and Australia with their Merino clip on three separate occasions rewarded their efforts. They also were awarded first prize at the Wembley Exhibition.

Rifle shooting was Hugh MacKenzie's passion and he held the opening rifle shoot annually at Walter Peak with between 80 to 130 people attending. Highland hospitality and generosity was par for the course in the MacKenzie homestead. Over the years they entertained distinguished guests from across the world and staged Scottish gatherings and conventions.

Hugh's wife Anastasia died in 1897 and he remarried Flora Gardiner when he was 58. He died in 1933 aged 84.

'The MacKenzies, perhaps more than any other family in New Zealand, lived practically as a clan, due no doubt to the combination of their ancestry and their isolation on the less accessible shore of the lake and when Hugh MacKenzie died at Dunedin in May 1933, the district mourned the passing of a chieftain. From the beginning he had been the head of the family, a position to which his resolute pioneering spirit and his integrity and generosity had justly entitled him. When he died, he left behind him a record of achievement that was full in keeping with the finest of pioneering traditions, for the Walter Peak station had by that time become one of the most famous in New Zealand.'

Excerpt from 'Golden Days of Lake Country' by F.W.G. Millar

His son Hugh had married and moved further away from the station, leaving only John and Alex, who were getting on in years and Peter who could not do manual work. Following the Depression the family were hit with severe winters of 1939, '43 and '45 and due to heavy losses decided to sell off Mt Nicholas and focus on Walter Peak itself.

Unfortunately for them the sale of Mt Nicholas and 15 000 sheep went through in 1949 to the Hunt's of Wanaka, just before the 1950-51 wool boom. The following year (1950) Alex passed away and John likewise in 1956. Only Colonel Peter was left as Hugh had relinquished his shares when Mt Nicholas was sold. Peter was the only one who had a son but he did not seem interested in running the station so when his two sisters died he decided it was time to end the MacKenzie era after 80 years and sold up in September 1960 to Cliff Heron of Balfour.

In 1967 George Wiles, an English Industrialist came on the scene – rumour had it that he was a self-made millionaire. He offered the Herrons over the odds for the property and the deal was struck in 1968. Mr Wiles was not from farming stock but had visited Molesworth Station once and was so taken with the huge numbers of cattle

that he decided to stock Walter Peak similarly. He also had huge development plans for the station in both farming and tourist ventures. Lavishly he built roads, stockyards and re-fenced for cattle, stocking over 2000 head by 1970. On the tourist side, George initiated the morning and afternoon teas for visitors at the homestead, who had travelled over on the TTS Earnslaw to the station. He converted the Colonel's House into a museum and the wool shed held shearing and sheep dog demonstrations.

He had great plans of building chalets and motels but unfortunately things turned to custard when money was running short and he floated his tourist venture on the open market as a company but attracted no takers. John Reid, a Dunedin stock and station agent took over in August 1972.

"You'll come out for a day or two on the autumn muster when the weather is a bit better," said John Templeton to me as he dropped us off at the jetty for the return journey to Queenstown.

Hill ground, Walter Peak

MOUNT NICHOLAS STATION

ount Nicholas Station, the largest run (41 000ha) in the Lake Wakatipu area, has an ideal location. It is only a twenty minute boat ride from Queenstown – the adventure Mecca of the world – with top restaurants, bars and other amenities, yet is secluded from the hordes of tourists, by the fact that the only road access is a two hour drive from Mossburn on a no exit, gravel road which is impassable for several months of the year.

As there are several creeks to be forded. I opted for the scenic drive past Mavora Lakes due to the TTS Earnslaw sailings not coinciding with my appointment. This route took me through over 30km of Mount Nicholas and part of the renowned neighbouring Walter Peak Station before reaching the shores of Lake Wakatipu, the station homestead and out houses, nestled in Whites Bay, with dark wooden woolshed, shearers' quarters and other assorted buildings along with the quay and mountain and lake backdrop – it was spectacular.

Only a few days before Christmas, Mount Nicholas Station owners – the Butson family were reunited: Robert and Linda had daughter Kate (a financial manager with the National Bank in Te Kuiti) and son David (who had been working on stations in Queensland) home for the festive season. With all staff: 2 shepherds, a cook and her handy man husband away on holiday – they had this piece of paradise to themselves. "It has been a great place to grow up and brilliant to come home to as there is so much to do and it is also close to Queenstown," said Kate, who with her brother David, was initially taught at home via correspondence.

"It was very sociable in these days as most of the lakeside stations were privately owned but over the years it has changed as the majority are now owned by overseas investors or Maori and there is not the same community spirit like there used to be," said Robert who moved to Mount Nicholas from Garston in 1976. He bought the property in partnership with his parents, Bill and Beatrice, who were earthmoving contractors. They had been friendly with the previous owners,

Phil and Judy Hunt who were retiring to Arrowtown, after 28 years on Mount Nicholas, and the Butsons were given the first option to buy the station.

"I'd always been a keen hunter, loved the hills, been farming and done a fair bit of mustering around Garston but running a station was a major learning curve. Peter Phipps, who had been head shepherd for the previous owner stayed on for two years and was a great help," explained Robert.

"The property had been well run, but needed a cash injection," stated Robert, "we were helped a lot by the fact the government had money available for development through the Rural Bank.

"Over the years we developed more than 10 000ha, over sowing ground up to 915m, which had all been covered in fern. McKellar Flat, which was native, was direct drilled with clover and cocksfoot. We changed breeds of both sheep and cattle and increased the sheep tally by two and a half times, but we are still not carrying as many sheep as Mount Nicholas did in its heyday,

The Butsons: Kate, Robert and David on Mount Nicholas Station.

when operated by the McKenzie family in conjunction with Walter Peak and Fern Hill Stations, before the 1940's rabbit explosion."

David McKellar, the first white man to set foot on the now Mount Nicholas Station in 1858, described the terrain he had surveyed to two Australians – the Hamilton brothers. They applied for this run but sold it soon after, preferring the country round Mavora Lakes.

The new owners were Englishmen from Nottinghamshire – John and Taylor White. They built their elaborate homestead about 12km from the lakefront and the cooks' stone cottage still stands there today. By 1867 the Whites were at loggerheads in a legal wrangle with their neighbours over the boundaries so due to expenses, multiplying rabbits and dwindling stock numbers they decided to cut their loses and sell up.

Over the next four decades a series of owners came and went, suffering loses due to severe weather conditions and rabbit infestation.

By 1904 Mount Nicholas had become part of the MacKenzie Kingdom (as mentioned in the Walter Peak chapter), as was Fernhill Station, until they sold out in 1949. The new owners – the Hunts were there until the present day owners – Robert and Linda Butson bought them out in 1976.

The Butsons have been cashing in on the tourism sector for over 16 years. They are shareholders in the Southern Lakes Heliski operation, which was initially established with well-known, local pilot, Richard 'Hannibal' Hayes.

"It is actually a great advantage in the winter as the pilots report back if they spot any animals in difficulty," says Robert.

A hunter through and through, Robert has been involved in a Wildlife Safari venture for the past twelve years. The outfit offers, 'a feast for the eyes and vitamins for the soul of any true hunter,' with all South Island species on offer on free range or safari hunts. The 80-year-old station homestead is home from home for the weary hunter after a day on the hills.

"I don't think tourism in the high country is the money maker that everyone thinks it is, but it is another interest," said Robert. "It gives us all something else to talk about other than farming," added Linda, "and we meet interesting people from all over the world."

When the Butsons arrived at Mount Nicholas, some 24 years ago, half-bred sheep were scaling the Hummocks and Thomson ranges. "Our aim was to produce adult Merinos of 22 micron," said Robert. "Breeding up from the halfbreds was a slow way to get Merinos but it appears to have worked in our favour as they seem to have a tolerance to foot rot."

Purchasing sires of 21 and 22 micron from the Matangi Stud at Little Valley and some from the Sutherland brothers of Benmore Station, which are incidentally both from Merrivale bloodlines, has resulted in the Butsons exceeding expectations by fleecing an average 20.5 micron off the adult flock this season. The hoggets average 18 micron with the finest at 16.8 micron.

Robert Butson keeps an eagle eye to avoid a smother.

Historically all the Mount Nicholas woolclip (some 115 000kgs) was sold at auction, but Robert, a strong supporter of contracts, has recently committed just over a third – 41 000kgs of 20.5 micron – to the Icebreaker label, for three years. "It has given us the stability to look into the future. When wool amounts to 75% of your income, you need something more stable to base budgets on," said Robert.

For the past 14 years, Mount Nicholas Station has shared a wool classer – Willis Arbuckle– with Nokomai Station. Tony Mooney preceded him for a decade before. To fit in with the classing, shearing contractor Peter Lyons, follows on from Nokomai Station with his gangs of Fernmark accredited shearers and wool handlers.

All 8200 adult ewes are run in one mob at tupping time, for a five-week period, with 2500 4-tooths in another mob. They are wintered on saved hill blocks and shorn with cover combs in late August. Prior to lambing they are capsule drenched and set stocked.

Weaning takes place in late January, with 2000 cull ewes being transferred to Fairlight Station – at the end of the Kingston Flier line – where they are shorn before heading off to the end of another line – the freezing works.

The main mob then moves onto the high country – the Hummocks – until the 13th of April. Their offspring are sexed, dipped and put on a regular monthly drenching program through the winter. With the increase in wool prices, a change of policy has been introduced: all cull lambs are grazed (at Fairlight) for another season to capitalise on the wool returns and are then placed on the market as 2-tooths. Selection is very much eye appeal with size and wool type being the deciding factors. "We try to run a big easy care operation and not get too scientific, with 35 000 stock units and only two men we need to keep things simple as the labour input is pretty low," he said.

Hoggets are shorn in late September and wethers in mid October. The wethers are put out in the summer country, up to 1830m on the Thomson Mountains, in late December until the Fall Muster on April 20th.

"We have tried to stay traditional by keeping horses in the system and are one of the few properties that still use horses on the annual muster. We are very much a horse family: breeding, breaking in and shoeing our own." Robert still leads the 6-man strong, 12-day muster as he has done for the past 24 years. "The shepherds just seem to get younger and fitter," he laughs.

Helicopters are used very rarely on Mount Nicholas compared to other stations, "but they are a great back up for sheep in trouble in snow," admits Robert, "and they have made high country farming easier and safer."

"I do admit that the area is a bit on the wet side for Merinos as they are not easy to run, being susceptible to foot rot and worms, but I do not know any other breed that can utilise the 41 000ha to the same degree. They are

Homesteads old and new.

Robert whistles to move on the sheep.

not the best Merinos in the country," he modestly claims, "but they preform well on our ground."

Conversion from black and whites to red and whites on the cattle front was a priority for the Butsons on their arrival to the station on the southern shores of Lake Wakatipu. "The Belted Galloways introduced by the Hunts, were hardy but the killing out percentage was less than desirable," commented Linda.

Robert opted for Herefords and has stuck to them even though the market has demanded exotics, as they can thrive on the rugged terrain. "They can get light in condition in winter as they can spend up to six weeks in a metre of snow but come back and still preform well on a low input system, explained Robert."

The 860 breeding cows are managed in a genuine run situation on the 3333ha McKellar Flat – named after the Scottish explorer and first white man to set foot on Mount Nicholas – David McKellar. It is very much an easy care

Hereford weaners on McKellar Flat.

system: they are completely left to their own devices, as they remain there from mating (40 cows to each bull), through calving in late September until weaning. The bulls are trucked out to the blocks as the property covers some 30km in length and other cows and calves are encountered en route.

Calving percentages vary from 85-90% from year to year and simplicity is again the rule with no pregnancy diagnosis carried out. Culling is aimed at cows in their 9th or 10th year.

The calves are weaned in late May, with the steers returning to McKellar Flat and the heifers trucked home to the developed country until they calve. Costs are cut on the health scene, as cattle are drenched twice a year until they turn 3 year old (while on the low ground) and never again. The breeding cattle are shifted into the Oreti Basin and mountain valleys of up to 1220m for the winter.

All steers are hung up at Alliance's Mataura plant with about 90% falling into the top grade

weighing around 275kgs. "We aim to kill in consignments of over 100 to utilise haulage costs. I'd like to think that in the future we can hold or increase production levels, but 20 years into a major development programme it is a struggle to hold position as far as stock numbers go."

Robert has an annual topdressing program and introduces a bit of seed every year. "The weather has become so violent with long dry spells, it is not easy to plan and monitor development."

With the micron fining up, he feels that the sheep appear to be harder to run and he'd rather hold on to micron and wool weights than increase production.

Mailbox

10000 sheep cross the North Von Bridge.

I returned to Mount Nicholas on the last day of their autumn muster, driving in the back road to the North Von Bridge. There I waited, watching an endless stream of lines of sheep dutifully following one another along the hillside tracks, across shingle faces, through low lying scrub and over the brow of the summit of the holding block. The white specs made the hillside come alive like a mass of maggots on a piece of meat.

As I watched, I heard a vehicle approaching – a Landrover – a welcome sight – made me feel quite at home. It was the packer – Matt Menlove. He had been clearing up in the South Von Hut where the musterers had spent the past few nights, "I heard you pass, you should have stopped in for a cup of tea," he said after we had introduced ourselves. "They'll be another hour yet before they are at the bridge," he said.

As man with ovine, canine and equine counterparts neared, the whistling, bleating, barking and whinnying sounds were ever prevalent, now competing with the soothing gush of the North Von River, as I sat on my prime camera shooting spot.

Finally horses, men and dogs were silhouetted on the horizon reminiscent of cowboys in the movies. They dismounted and led their steed's downhill, with dogs obediently at heel, as the last of the mob hurtled down the hillside.

Robert Butson crossed the bridge, grinning and greeted me as he changed the gates ready for the crossing. Once the initial few made a break across the overpass he positioned himself on the banking so they would not come with a rush. The shepherds; David Butson, James Crutchley, Pat McNamee, Cameron Scott and Dean Tomlinson, worked in the background keeping the sheep flowing at a steady pace. I didn't have a watch but they must have been crossing for at least 45 minutes.

Leaving my car at the bridge, I joined Robert

Going home after a 10 day muster.

and Pat McNamee and followed the tail end of the mob the last 15km into the station. Pat, well up in his fifties, was on his twentieth muster, he farms at Five Rivers and has been friends with Robert for years.

With Robert setting off at a canter, dogs in hot pursuit, to help sort out a blockage in the mob ahead, I was left in the company of Pat McNamee. One of the old school, Pat certainly knew what he was about and kept me informed and amused during our trek back to the station.

Every now and then Pat would say, "Hello there Josh," and I thought he was trying to get through to someone on the handheld radio, which the musterers use for contact, to keep abreast of the action. It took me some time to realise that Josh was one of Pat's dogs and he was just letting him know that he was well aware that he was doing something he wasn't meant to! As we were pretty much following the end of the mob and the dog work was close at hand, Pat was using voice commands rather than the usual whistling. "Hoi, Bruce your name's not Mist!" was one of my favourites as was, "Come in here, Josh, Bruce, Mist, whoever you are!"

We came upon a wether, which was shaking and had collapsed in the tussock – I presumed from sheer exhaustion, but Pat knew otherwise and quickly whipped out his knife. I reckoned he was going to slit the throat as a dog tucker but he had instantly diagnosed Tutu poisoning and cut a slit down the side of the face, to prevent the wether from dying from blood poisoning.

Reaching the descent to the homestead and lakeside was the view, as a photographer, I had been waiting for, as for most of the walk in we couldn't see the whole mob ahead of us. Coming down the hillside with the picturesque panorama of the Lake Wakatipu, the surrounding mountains and **ten thousand sheep** was for me, a Scottish West Coast Highlander, unreal.

Once in the lane way about half the mob were diverted into a paddock while the rest went on down to the yards on the lakeside. The

Pat McNamee with horses and dogs.

shepherds brushed down and rugged up their horses and fed their dogs before they made off to the quarters. I was taken to the cook shop for a cup of tea.

Pat, who had told me earlier that he was going to head home immediately, decided he was going to have a shower when he heard that I was catching a ride back to my car at the North Von bridge. "I wasn't given an option, Pat told me I had to have a shower as a young lady was coming in the truck with us," laughed Matt Menlove.

After a few swift rums at the homestead with the Butsons, we headed off. Pat took the pair of us back to his house at Five Rivers, where his wife Barbara served up a dinner of vast proportions, rounding off another wonderful day in the high country.

Robert Butson thanks casual shepherd Cameron Scott as he drops him and his 6 dogs off in Queenstown.

Ninety Mile Beach, Te Paki Station, Cape Reinga.

North Island Stations

Waipu

Araparawanui

Pipi Bank

A Scottish welcome in New Zealand.

THE SETTLERS
OF WAIPU

One of the most epic tales of New Zealand immigrants of Scottish descent must be the saga of the 800 or so followers of the Rev Norman MacLeod. This preacher and his congregation left Assynt in the West Highlands of Scotland in 1817 and headed for Cape Bretton, Nova Scotia, where they pioneered and set up a lively community. But winters were long and harsh and after over 30 years in this colony they decided to move on, led by the minister who was now well into his seventies.

With many able seamen and fishermen in their midst they built their own ships and sailed initially to Australia and then to New Zealand. By 1860, 6 ships had arrived at Auckland: the Margaret, the Highland Lass, the Gertrude, the Spray, the Bredalbane and the Ellen Lewis with these intrepid Scottish Highland travellers on board. They finally set up home around the village of Waipu in Northland.

Ross Finlayson, who farms 3000 acres at Purua, is a descendant of pioneers who originally set sail from the Kyle of Lochalsh in Wester Ross.

He has travelled to both Nova Scotia and Scotland and still has distant relations at the village of Plockton, north of Kyle, made famous internationally following the release of the TV series, Hamish MacBeth.

The Finlaysons' holding is not a station as such, like all the other properties covered in this book, but I thought the story of the settlers of Waipu was too unique and classic to miss out.

Milking 920 Friesian cows is a far cry from the initial stocking rates in the far north, as once the trees were removed the soils were impoverished. Some time passed before this area was developed into productive farmland.

As with most New Zealand dairy farms, the Finlaysons dry all the cows off over the winter period. "But for 40 years we did milk every day of the year as we were on town supply," explains Ross who has been farming the property for over fifty years.

Latterly Ross has taken a back seat and his youngest son Ken has been at the helm, as overseer of the 6 fulltime, staff for the past 8

years. Ken plans to study history at Auckland University. His brother John is an agricultural scientist and received a doctorate for his work on the greenhouse effect on Scottish Agriculture and is now an economist in Hamilton. The third son is a vet in Manilla.

The cattle are grazed on rotation in 5 acre paddocks, moved on to fresh grass after each milking in two herringbone milking sheds, a 20 aside and a 12 aside, which are run simultaneously in the height of the season. Milk production is targeted at 16 000litres/cow/annum.

All cows are Artificially Inseminated and then covered by Hereford bulls. "We have used Prostaglandin but it is not a regular part of our practice. We dry off on the 15th May and start calving on 15th July."

"We sell the male calves at a week old, most for rearing and the heifers are reared on the property," says Ross.

"Maize silage and turnips are normally grown, but the past 2 years have been so good and the silage pits are still full so there are no crops in this year. It is the best season I can remember," he avows, as we tour round the property.

We stop at some drainage ditches and Ross explains to me that when his Great Uncle, Angus Finlayson, bought the property in conjunction with some Auckland businessmen in 1907 the land was part of the Hikurangi swamp. They dug a hole and installed a coal-fired, steam powered dredge which was used to create a canal to the Wairau river some three miles away. Up to 80 Maoris were employed to dig contributory drains.

Ross's ancestors had been skilled bushmen in the forests of Nova Scotia and they used their skills here in New Zealand to earn a living and raise the capital to buy farmland. These bush workers were physically 'fit as fiddles' and showed their prowess on the athletics field at the Waipu Highland Games – an annual event which is held to this day.

One of Ross's uncles – Norman Finlayson of Maungaturoto– had six sons, who made their mark in New Zealand Rugby. The game of rugby was only in its very early years in the Far North when the boys were young, but the 1905 All Blacks Tour of the UK had given New Zealand Rugby the edge.

Three of the boys: Jack, Bain and Owen (Tote) were signed up for the First World War and all three made it into the seven-aside team that represented the Auckland Regiment in Egypt and won the brigade championship. Two of them made the team who were champion division of New Zealand.

Another brother – Innes – aka 'Bunny' went on to be an All Black and is renown as 'one of the greatest players the country has produced.'

Four of the brothers – Tote, Bain, Angus and Bunny – represented North Auckland on the same day. Angus later played for Auckland for many years, while Callum, another of the firebound Finlaysons, captained the province of Otago for two of the eight seasons when he was a member of that side.

Jack Finlayson later became President of the New Zealand Rugby Union.

Dairy cows

Bulk fert spreading

Ross Finlayson, whose ancestors came out from Kyle of Lochalsh.   *Some of the draining done by Ross's forebears.*

ARAPARAWANUI

Not all settlers who took up land in Aotearoa had been farming in their homeland. John McKinnon of the Isle of Lewis, the largest island in the Scottish Western Isles, is one colonizer who went to sea as a lad of thirteen. Born in 1823 to Angus and Ann (nee MacFarlane) McKinnon, who were married in Stornoway on 21st January the preceding year, this young lad found his sea legs and over the next twelve years went on to obtain his first mate's and master's certificates.

At the time there were only two McKinnon families (not connected) in Lewis and rumour has it that these McKinnons were run off the Isle of Skye for sheep stealing.

One story John McKinnon enjoyed telling in later years was of when the 'Mary Florence' became ship wrecked off the coast of Africa, and all aboard had to jump ship. The seas were high and the lifeboats overturned in the surf. Seven were drowned, including the captain and his wife, leaving only John McKinnon and two others.

On reaching dry land they were taken prisoner by African tribesmen who marched them inland and tied them to a stake at their camp. Apparently, the mate and the seaman were 'eaten by cannibals', but the hardy Western Islander managed to escape one night and headed for the coast. Four months later he was picked up by a passing ship and landed at Aden.

Following a stint working for the East India Company and then a couple of years on the steamboats on the Mississippi River, he returned to Lewis and married Mary Catherine (Kate) McIver of Stornoway. Their first child, Catherine (Kate), was born at Stornoway on 23 May 1853.

Early 1854, John sailed from Dundee for Melbourne as mate on the "Kossuth", leaving his new bride behind, carrying their second child. Apparently Catherine found deeds to land that John had bought on the banks of the Mississippi and burnt them, having no intention of settling in America.

From Australia, this intrepid traveller headed for New Zealand as mate on the brig 'Kirkwood'.

At Wairoa he was given command of the 40-tonne schooner "Wave" but left the sea shortly after and went saw milling for a while.

By 1856 he was appointed pilot for the Port of Napier, a post he held for two years, in which time he brought the port's first paddle steamer the 'Wonga-Wonga', and also the first English ship into harbour .

John decided that he would make New Zealand home so wrote asking his wife to come out. At first she refused, saying she did not want to live in a country with cannibalism, to which John replied that if she did not come he would marry a Maori woman. Needless to say, Catherine was on the next boat out – the 'Oliver Lang' accompanied by her youngest brother, Murdoch MacIver, and her two daughters; Catherine and Mary Ann (b. 8/9/1854).

John McKinnon took up about 5000 acres of land on the coast north of Napier in 1863, an isolated spot at the mouth of the Aropaoanui River. He named it 'Arapawanui', miss-spelling the original Maori name.

Araparawanui.

At the mouth of Brooking's Gully,
  On a terrace clean and dry,
Where we used to boil the billy,
  In the years that's long gone by.

There among the scrub and bushes,
  And the wild pigs in the fern,
Cleared away the logs and rushes,
  Pitch'd the tent and slept till dawn.

On this spot we built the station,
  For to guard our little flock,
Against the wild dog's inclination,
  Prowling up among the rocks.

The flock has grown, so has the station,
  As the years went rolling on,
Beautifying the situation,
  On every side you look upon.

Around a pool of clear water,
  Under overhanging trees,
Climbing vines and twining creepers,
  Where the ladies make the tea.

Some are sitting in an arbour,
  Underneath the fig tree shade,
Squeezing lemons into water,
  Making up the lemonade.

A merry brook runs down the gully,
  From the limestone rocks behind,
Where the land is rather hilly,
  Where the woodhen shelter find.

Tumbling o'er the rocky boulders,
  Through the garden running clear,
Meandering on towards the river,
  Where it ends it's wild career.

JOHN McKINNON, Arapawanui, 1902

The MacKinnons left their mark.

Driving down the twisty road through forestry plantations, which seem to be one-a-penny in the Gisborne Region, it was a welcome vista to turn a sharp bend and be greeted with the green valley of Arapawanui below.

Unfortunately it is the only station on my travels that I did not meet the owner or manager and have a tour round the property. A bit rushed for time I could not get a hold of anyone at such short notice.

John and Catherine McKinnon went on to have another 7 children: Angus (b. 1859) and John (b. 1861) who were both born at Clive, with Donald (b. 23/5/63), Isabella (13/1/65), William and his still-born twin (b. Christmas Day 1869), Norman (b. 27/1/71) and Joanna (b.26/6/73) all born at Arapawanui.

The only access to the station, apart from by sea, was that of a coastal bridle track. The ocean transported wool and heavy goods. One year while loading his wool onto the ship, the mate told him that the captain had died at sea and they had to secure a skipper for the voyage back to England. McKinnon struck up a deal with the agents, that he would take the ship back if they would fell a block of bush on his run and put it into pasture as well as provide stores for his family. A year later when he returned, he found that the arrangement had been honoured.

During the land wars, which flared through Taranaki and the East Coast from 1866 to 1872, European settlers living on isolated farms, in the province, went in daily fear of surprise attack, as the authorities found it difficult to give them any warning. In 1869, John Powdrell, a youngster from the Wairoa District, was returning home from Napier on the racehorse, 'Queen of the Vale', when he was stopped by the Military and told of Te Kooti's attack on Mohaka (10/4/69). He was asked to take a detour to warn the McKinnon family before returning to Napier to report the attack.

The horses had been turned out and Mrs McKinnon and the children left on foot with John Powdrell, while Mr McKinnon hid the family valuables. As he was leaving to look for the horses, he heard a stramash in the hen house and found three Maoris helping themselves to the hens. He managed to persuade them to go.

A few hours later, John McKinnon, accompanied by as many horses as he could muster, caught up with his family en route to Pentane, where they slept in the loft over the stables of a packed out hotel.

The McKinnon family were lucky to return to find their farmhouse and out houses intact, as many other settlers to the North of Napier had their homesteads burnt to the ground.

In 1886, John McKinnon took up more land – a Crown leasehold property on the coast and six years later he purchased Moeangiangi Estate – some 5000 acres of freehold and 5000 acres leasehold along with 13 000 sheep for $15 000.

As he grew older, John McKinnon enjoyed spending more time sitting by the river writing poetry. His native homeland – the Isle of Lewis and his New Zealand valley were favourite topics for him to pen. One he wrote for his Golden Wedding, which they celebrated with friends and family on Christmas Day 1898 follows.

JUBILEE POEM

Fifty years are gone and past,
And many friends have gone to rest,
And many more have been dispersed
Since Kate and I were wed.
In the village by the sea,
With sunny aspect warm and free,
There sweetly blows the ocean breeze
Where Kate was born and bred.

That village, once a jewel bright,
A beacon star in winter night,
The weary mariner to enlight,
Approaching from the sea.
The hardy fishermen were brave,
Boarding ships on the stormy wave,
And guide them into Stornoway.
Before a lighthouse on Arnish Point,
Nor beacon on the rock.

Where are those bold pilots now?
Alas! They're buried in the ground,
Their children scattered the world around,
Their houses levelled to a mound
    To make room for farmers' sheep
    And lowland cattle fat and sleek,
    Grazing in the very street
    Where once Holm village stood.

Oh Holm how I love to dwell,
When down to court my bonnie belle,
I took a stroll at eventide,
Just to while away the time,
    The kindly faces I did see
    In that village by the sea.
Remembrance of the time of old
Of stories by the fireside told.

Now my tale proceed along,
Relate the burden of my song;
    The road is rough, the journey long,
    That covers all the thorny paths
    That I have travelled in the past,
    The years gone by are like the shade,
    From the memory they fade.

Looking through the mist of years,
When we were young and scant of wealth,
We faced the future without fear,
    Strong in courage, hope and health.
My profession was upon the sea,
    A roving sailor's life,
I travelled far by sea and land,
I left behind my wife.

To Torrid Zone and Artic cold
    I'd sail the sea's along,
I worked and strove to earn some gold,
    My luck went always wrong.
In gales and tempests toss'd about,
    The good ship tight and sound,
Or cast ashore on savage coast,
    The breakers all around.

In fevered climes I was sometimes
    By sickness tired sore,
Almost crushed the hope devine,
    Of going home once more.
My visits back to see my bride,
    Like a comet through the sky,
Were very few and far between,
    I left her with a sigh.

For ten long years I wandered
    To countries far and wide,
I often thought and wondered
    How Providence provide.
I stumbled on the Maoriland,
    In the far off Southern Sea,
I looked around the fertile ground,
    And planted my rooftree.

I camp'd upon the riverbank,
    Among the forest trees,
I cooed for my dove to come
    And settle here with me.
And here through weal and woe we toiled
    For forty years and more,
In this valley by the side,
Of the river's rippling ford.

Among a people bold and free,
The New Zealanders of yore,
Who lived in these Southern climes
    Before we seen their shore.

JOHN McKINNON,
NAPIER, NEW ZEALAND, 1898

In the valley of the Moangi
    Where the river's running clear,
Between hills of passing grandeur,
    Rising in the ranges near.

When in flood it met the ocean
    With a roar and mighty bound,
The surf beating on the shore
    In the commotion all around.

The scene is changed to the westward,
    Where the hills are rock-fast bound
Where the wild pig and the rabbit
    Find a cavern from the hound.

Where the Tutira Valley
    Is running parallel with the sea,
With its lake of limped water
    Rippling to the mountain breeze.

Down the Glen of Pawanui,
    Where the sun rise in the morn;
Where the Clan McKinnon settled,
    Pioneers who hold their own.

Long may live that clan together
    In a friendly loving way,
Is the prayer of the founder
    Of that Clan in early days.

JOHN MCKINNON
Stornoway, 27th September. 1910.

Homestead gardens

Catherine McKinnon (74) died on 12 December 1902, after a long illness, being nursed by their daughter Isabella (Bella). A Gaelic inscription on the tombstone has been translated as: "As long as the family of McKinnon remember their mother and family come from the land of the mountains."

In 1903 John McKinnon and Bella sailed to Scotland and again in 1904, leaving sons Angus and William at the helm of Arapawanui. John (jnr.) was farming Karamu and Kaihunahuna, Norman on Stratholm and Donald on Moeangiangi. John McKinnon remarried in Glasgow, on 22 August 1904 – Christina Murray – a widow with five children. He was aged 84 and she just 38. He built a new house at 8 Newton Street (apparently where all the retired sea captains live) for his new bride and was referred to by the locals as 'the millionaire'.

John McKinnon died on 13th November 1912, in Stornoway, aged 89. That same year a road was constructed between Tongoio and the Aropaoanui River, making it possible for vehicles to reach the station for the first time. The freehold at Arapawanui was divided in 1912 equally between Angus and William. Angus kept the name and William named his block –

Glendale, possibly after where the Clan McKinnon originally came from on Skye.

No McKinnon's are left at Arapawanui but several descendants are still farming in Hawkes Bay. I met up with Brian McKinnon, a great grandson of John McKinnon and grandson of the second son, also John (jun) who came to farm at Karamu.

Mrs McKinnon had the family history well documented and kindly gave me a photocopy. Following a hearty meal and chat about Scotland, where they have visited on several occasions we got down to the nitty gritty of genealogy and family trees.

These McKinnon descendants farm some 2000 acres north of Wairoa with beef cattle and sheep. They also grow 16ha of sweetcorn, which is used as a 90-day rotation crop, for Heinz Wattie.

Homestead Araparawanui.

Dry and dusty yards as sheep are loaded for the works.

PIPI BANK

On the coast, just south of Cape Turnagain, lies Pipi Bank Station, the southern most coastal property in Hawkes Bay.

Perthshire born Speedys; John, William and Graham came out with other siblings and their parents, David and Helen, from Forebrae, Methven aboard the Lord William Bentinick' in 1841. Initially the family settled in the Hutt Valley and began farming with just two cows.

The Speedy boys flew the nest with William and Graham working as shepherds near Wellington.

Extracts from a letter from the Wellington sheep farmer to his brother in Scotland in 1849, made the pages of The New Zealand Journal (London).

We have been very fortunate with servants as yet. We have two brothers , shepherds at our out station, from Perthshire. Their father was a small farmer in the neighbourhood of Perth – David Speedy. The eldest we have had for about 2 years – he now receives his £30 a year and rations. The younger is about 14 – he gets 7s a week and feed. Now these are the people who better their condition by coming out and instead of £10 or £12 a year at home, with oatmeal three times a day, they get these large wages with meat, flour and tea at every meal – in fact they enjoy the run of the pantry.

The lads went on to work for Thomas Guthrie on Castlepoint Station. Guthrie's wife was Anne Groves. Her brother John came out to Castlepoint in 1855 and set up a trading post, providing accommodation for travellers. The Alexander Turnbull Library has letters from John Groves in the archives.

The liquor we sell is astonishing. There is hardly one but takes one or two bottles with them. All that travel on horse back has got two large leather bags hanging to their saddle and some of them will carry six bottles in them. There was one here last Wednesday that carried 12 bottles in his saddle bags. Rum and Gin is 5/- per bottle…this is a dreadful country for drink.

Helen Speedy was widowed in 1858 and was probably the first female farmer in New Zealand. She ran 270 sheep, a horse, 7 pigs, 36 hens, 16 cows half an acre of oats and one and a half acres of potatoes on 600 acres near Wellington. She sold the produce; butter, cheese, eggs, potatoes, bacon, hay, wool and beef locally and also had some shipped out to John Groves at Castlepoint. Two of her sons – William and Graham - went on to marry Guthrie's nieces – Fanny and Emily Groves.

By 1856 sheep scab was a major problem in the Wairarapa and William Speedy was appointed 'Inspector of Sheep' for the area from 1857 to 1861. His remit was to visit every sheep farm biannually.

In the late 1850's the three brothers bought land on the south side of the Wainui River, near Cape Turnagain from where Captain Cook turned round years earlier.

They named their 10 000 acre property Pipi Bank due to the huge numbers of pipi shells found in layers in the sand banks.

A clay hut was built and by 1860 there were 2000 sheep on Pipi Bank. The three brothers split the holding in 1874. John who had established his own 1550 strong flock named his portion Burnbank, Graham set up Woodbank, while William remained at the original station homestead.

I journeyed down one sunny, blustery day and caught up with William and Ngaire Speedy who presently manage Pipi Bank. The Station, which has a 5km beach front, now covers 1017ha with some forestry on the hill ground and 200ha of sand dunes and marram grass.

Historically the sheep on Pipi Bank were Merinos but with an average rainfall of 42" it was considered rather wet. "When my father was a teenager they ran Lincolns but the hoggets died like flies," exclaimed Bill Speedy.

"We were running 4000 Romneys but reduced to 3300 ewes when the forestry was planted. Border Leicesters were used about 20 years ago to open up the faces," explained Bill as he pushed some sheep heading for slaughter up a dusty race.

"We sell most as store, privately off the place, as quite frankly the store market has been ahead of the works price anyway. They have you over a barrel at Dannevirke yards if the price is not good."

"The last 7 to 8 years have been tough for hill farmers so there are just the two of us but fortunately we get on," said Bill grinning at his outbreaks of Toxoplasmosis and Camplyobacter.

John Speedy and his dog.

wife Ngaire across the table.

The couple muster the sheep using 4WD bikes, taking care on the steep country which rises from sea level to 900 feet. "I like to do the lambing on horse back, but if the weather is bad it is an easy care system and they get on with it."

Lambing percentages at Pipi Bank have been around 125% but dropped to 110% recently with outbreaks of Toxoplasmosis and Camplyobacter.

Bill has made several changes on Pipi Bank since he started working at home with his father, Spencer, in 1953. He has subdivided blocks into more paddocks, extended the area which is fertilised and planted pines in conjunction with a company from Singapore.

The first cattle on the station were Shorthorns and Bill's grandfather used to barter the milk in exchange for goods. These days 260 Angus x

Hereford cattle, 150 weaners and 60 rising 2 year old replacements, graze the slopes and flats on this Hawkes Bay holding.

"We have problems with eye cancer with the Herefords in the North Island so are turning back to the pure Angus."

"The key to this country is that we have good water. We have spent money over the years digging out springs and have two streams that are

Looking down on the station and Cape Turnagain.

117

BURNVIEW
STATION

WARNING!

never dry. The downside is erosion in some places," said Bill.

"Slips are difficult to fence in the steep country. We have two paddocks which can only be subdivided by electric fencing over the slip ground. We use No. 7 wire and Totra posts because of the coastal erosion – good Scots methods – 'waste nothing.'

The biggest earthquake in New Zealand was off Cape Turnagain in 1855, it raised the coastline by 8 feet. Graham Speedy who had been driving stock around the coast from Wellington with another man, stopped in to visit the lighthouse keeper at Pencarrow. Barrels of flour and oil rolled around during the earthquake and blocked the door, trapping them inside. Graham noted that prior to the earthquake sheep could only be moved round rocks at Mukamuka at low tide but following the quake it was possible to drove them round at high tide.

Having personally encountered an earthquake in New Zealand – 5.6 on the Richter Scale – I can say it was the most terrifying experience ever.

The Speedy brothers were instrumental in inventing and setting up wool presses. William applied for a wool press patent in 1874. His invention was mounted on a sledge and used ropes, chains or bands instead of the usual screw for pressing.

John Speedy came out with a different version four years later. His prototype used a large wheel rotating through cogs and a pair of axles on either side of the press which pulled chains attached to the moving head.

On his retirement, William applied for another patent for the 'William Speedy's Double Acting Lever Wool Press.' 'The motive power from the levers was transmitted through a double acting ratchet assembly to iron bars connected to the moveable top.

William married Fanny Groves in 1859. She died in 1878 and he remarried Matilda Thorn Campbell. There were seven children from the first marriage and five from the second.

As the most Southern property in Hawkes Bay, Pipi Bank bounded with the Wairapapa. When rabbit infestations were prominent in the 1890's, the Hawkes Bay Rabbit Board erected a bunny-proof fence from the Waimata Stream to the Manawatu Gorge. The remains of the rabbit fence on Pipi Bank can be viewed extending into the sea in the photograph on page .

William died aged 62 in 1894. His two oldest sons leased the Station from trustees till David Graham – DG Speedy – purchased it in 1905. He married Catherine Bain Buchanan. His only son – Spencer (father of the present Speedy) – was next in line to run Pipi Bank.

Burnview Homestead

One of the first buildings on Pipi Bank

Remains of boundary fence

WALTER PEAK MUSTER

Returning from my North Island adventure mid April, later than anticipated, I was a bit concerned that I had missed any chance of getting on a high country muster, but Sharon Templeton, who assists her husband John in the management of Walter Peak Station assured me that I could join the muster when they moved to the Whiteburn Hut a couple of days later.

On my way to Mossburn I stopped in to see an old friend with whom I'd rousied (wool handled) on my first visit to New Zealand and subsequently shorn with in Scotland and on the Isle of Man. Jacqui (nee Coles) is now married to Wayne Ingram, who until recently held the two-stand shearing record with Darin Forde.

I set out from Jacqui's mid afternoon and headed in the back road to Walter Peak Station on shingle roads. Although I had already been in this way to interview at Mount Nicholas Station just before Christmas, I still soaked in the amazing scenery as if it had been the first time.

I drove up to the first hut I came to, but realised that it was the South Von Hut belonging to Mount Nicholas Station, so carried on down the road. Following Sharon's directions I soon spotted a wisp of smoke wafting above some trees to the right and cut off the road onto a track. There, round a bend on the bank of a river lay a nest of corrugated iron huts. A group of shepherds were lying stretched out in front of the largest hut enjoying a beer while another chopped meat for dog tucker in the foreground.

As a stranger in the camp I made my way towards them coyly but was soon surrounded by familiar faces: John Templeton manager of Walter Peak, Grant McMaster the packer (cook) who is the publican from Disasters in Waikaia and Cameron Scott who had been mustering and working at Nokomai Station.

"Here have a beer, Eilidh," said John Templeton as he introduced me to the others: full time shepherds, Mark Stalker and Hamish McKnight and casual shepherd Hamish Macdonald from Te Anau. As the evening wore on I found that I had shorn in Mark's uncle's shed near Mossburn, knew Hamish McKnight's mother and sister and had previously met the other Hamish while I had been watching Ben Hore velvet his deer at Waikaia.

As the temperature dropped we moved inside. I joined Grant in the cook shop, which was deceivingly much classier on the inside than it appeared from the exterior. "The cook shop has recently been renovated," explained Grant, "there used to be bunks in here too but they have been moved into the larger hut – what a difference!" he exclaimed. A wood-burning Aga had been installed for cooking but also doubled up for heating the water for a rustic outdoor shower.

As Grant and I chatted, he added some herbs to the chops in the huge camp stove on the Aga. Just then the lid fell off and half the contents fell in, he laughed and seemed completely unperturbed. Each musterer that came into the hut in turn said, "hmm smells good!" – as it did. Eventually everyone came into the cookhouse and sat round the table yarning and enjoying a few beers – SPEIGHTS of course being in Southland.

Homeward bound

Grant seems to be the ideal packer as his culinary skills were on a par with his wit – first class. Last time I had seen him in action was as MC at his brother in law's wedding in December. The chops were tender, accompanied by potato wedges and veges the meal was just top drawer – it was well seen why this packer was in demand. Grant now in his third season cooking for the Walter Peak muster also packs at Glenaray.

One by one the musterers disappeared for showers and then to bed. I was given a bed in the hut but I'm not sure if I actually slept at all that first night as every time someone got up for the toilet I thought it was time to get up! With breakfast call at 3.30am, everyone huddled round the table in numbed silence until the curried beans took immediate effect. All the musterers hoed into lashings of bacon, eggs and the dreaded curried beans while I opted for some cereal not being able to face a fry up at such an unearthly hour.

About 4am with dogs, hill sticks and cut lunches on board Cameron; aka 'Cameroon' or sometimes just 'Roon' to his cohorts, bump started the truck down the hill – we were mobile but in darkness! The trip to the South Von was eventful to say the least with Mark hanging out the window with a torch to guide the way and Hamish and I in the back just hoping the pair in front could see more than we could. Descending a rocky gorge on a ribbon of a track with one rear light on the ute (pickup) in front as a lead was no mean feat for the driver and a bit of a roller-coaster ride for us passengers.

Delighted to reach our destination in one piece, all and sundry clambered out ready for action. By 4.30am we were hoofing it by torchlight in single file. Mark Stalker, full-time shepherd on Walter Peak took the lead followed by yours truly, who obviously hadn't gone to guides as she was completely unprepared with no torch and modelling running shoes as the most suitable footwear available and cropped track pants! Casual musterer Cameron Scott was close on my heels shadowed by ex-rodeo rider Hamish Macdonald and a total of nineteen dogs following their respective owners.

At first I found walking across the slopes hard going in the semi-darkness until Cameron showed me how to use my hill stick to it's full potential. Initially I had been using it as I would a cromag or shepherds' crook at home, in an upright position as a lever and a support, but on tussocky and shingly terrain my Highland heather and moorland tactics were futile. "Hold it with both hands with the lower end facing the upper slope and dig it in and lean on it when necessary to give you support," he said.

Putting it in practice was hard at first, but later in the day I had mastered it to a certain degree and found it helped considerably especially on steep descents and traversing shingle (scree) or deep tussocky areas where visibility was poor.

The guys were great and didn't push me too hard. After a couple of hours, Mark and

Shepherds enjoy a beer after a hard day on the hill.

Chief cook and bottle washer – Grant McMaster

Cameron who were going to tackle the tops left Hamish and I. We carried on for a while until Hamish told me he was going up a difficult route and suggested an alternative for me where I could take my time and meet him on the horizon.

I ambled zigzagging up the face taking in my surroundings: the early morning light appearing with a pink tinge on Jane Peak (6530feet) across the creek on Mt Nicholas Station, huge snow tussocks, interspersed with Spaniards – long green leafed plants with razor sharp points at the end of each leaf which caused merry hell drawing blood on my bare legs. So that is possibly one reason the shepherds all wear gaiters coming to just below the knee I pondered as I spotted fresh sheep droppings and tracks in the shingle just below the ridge I was nearing.

Once on the top I sat down to enjoy the view and have a bit of a breather. I'd heard a bark up across on the next ridge and could see the matchstick silhouette of a shepherd on the horizon and scanned the slopes below for sheep movement. I find the Merinos much harder to spot than the Scottish Blackface or even crossbred sheep – while intact the merino fleece appears much darker than other breeds and thus makes it more difficult to see them. Below the cacophony of barks I eventually spied a string of sheep tearing across the slope in absolute terror.

Just then I heard a noise nearer at hand, a bit like galloping horses and noticed three beasts, which I initially presumed were deer, careering across the relatively level plateau towards me. Sitting on the edge of a precipice I was ever so slightly concerned about my safety as they came to a halt less than two metres from my feet, obviously having not spotted me. It was uncanny, I was closer to these beasts, which I could now see on closer inspection were not deer, than most hunters get in a lifetime. They had light fawn coloured markings down the side of their faces, reminded me of badgers' stripes a bit and also light markings round their rears. The only wildlife name that came to mind was thar – a wild goat, but they didn't really look like goats.

I sat motionless for a while in absolute awe at this spectacle, but as I slowly reached into my bag for my camera, they took fright and made off leaping down the shingle below me. Luckily a fourth one appeared but as I had moved it was aware of my presence and posed amiably for pictures before hissing at me, taking off up the ridge and periodically stopping and watching me, snorting in disgust as I had separated him from his mates.

As he disappeared from view Hamish came into sight with his seven dogs close on heel. I excitedly told him of my close encounters and from my description he reckoned I had seen chamois. From the Collins Concise Dictionary: chamois 1.a sure-footed goat of Europe and SW Asia, having vertical horns with backward pointing tips. 2 soft suede leather formerly made from this animal, now obtained from the skins of sheep and goats. 3 Also called chamois leather a piece of such leather used for polishing.

My Granny MacDonald always had the latter in her car and we as kids always made sure the windows were clear as her driving was notoriously bad!

Keeping in touch with procedures by radio Hamish decided we had time for a break as we were on the lower beat. Hamish told me that his grandfather came out to New Zealand from the Isle of Skye, with his family, when he was eight. Following the war he was balloted some land at Te Anau, where Hamish now farms in conjunction with his father Brian.

Hamish has only been home for just on 18 months following a ten-year stint in Canada where he competed in the Rodeo circuit each summer and managed a feedlot in the winter. Considering he has only been home for such a short time he has his dogs working extremely well. My favourite was Blitz, a huge huntaway who lived up to his name. Hamish was glad it

Enjoying the craic in the musterers hut.

who lived up to his name. Hamish was glad it was nearing the end of the muster, "I came straight from mustering on the McKenzies' Braemar Station near Mt Cook so the dogs are tired. This ground is really hard on their feet and they can lose pads," he said.

We dropped down across the shingle to follow in the wake of some sheep Hamish had hunted earlier. I put my newfound stick techniques into practice but struggled to keep up with the fit shepherd and his team of dogs on this foreign terrain, getting caught up in a forest of the dreaded Spaniards managing to catch up every time he stopped for a bark up or such like.

Eventually we hit the fence line with a couple of hundred sheep ahead of us, around lunchtime, and met up with the other two shepherds who had already pushed their mob through the gate. All in all, our contingent had gathered around 1200 wethers. John Templeton, Hamish McKnight and Graham Spittle (a local farmer who was out for the day) alias 'Dusty' had taken a different route and were still out on their beat.

Once we reached the trucks, Cameron made off for Queenstown as he was joining the Mount Nicholas muster the following day, while Hamish, Mark and I headed back to the hut with our charges.

The packer – Grant McMaster – was prepared and had cheese toasties at the ready which Sharon and Max (Mark's girlfriend) dished up as Grant had run Cameron to the boat. Even though I'd hardly covered half the distance of the boys I was absolutely exhausted that evening.

John and the rest of the tribe arrived about an hour after us having mustered the bulk of the mob, totalling around 6000 wethers now.

When everyone was still eating I chanced having a wash in the shower with the million-dollar view of the stars. Pre-warned re the temperature and not too put the hot tap on too far – I enjoyed the luxury of the hot water considering I had always heard stories of shepherds having to wash in freezing creeks.

*Hamish Macdonald keeps in touch
with the 2-way radio.*

Moving the mob.

Hamish and Matt watch on.

Last leg of the muster - over the Saddle and down to the Walterr Peak yards.

The water nipped my legs, which were suffering from my battles with Spaniards, but it was minor detail. The outdoor toilet or dunny also had a fantastic view of the stars but as it was a long drop the odours seemed to linger and visits there were short and sweet.

Woken by the generator at 5am the next day, which wasn't quite so anti-social, we grouped round the table for the last time. My buddies from the previous day – Hamish and Mark were to carry on and take the whole mob over the saddle to the station while the others were heading for the yards and had a few days drenching in front of them. I opted to help Grant pack up. We started in the bunkhouse and loaded the swags, packs and other shepherds' paraphernalia, then the food and cooking utensils followed by the generator and water pump.

We said our farewells and for me it was the end of an amazing experience: a couple of days' insight to the lifestyle of high country mustering. Reckon I'll have to get my hill boots sent over from Scotland or invest in a new pair and go into training!

Passing base camp.

Lake Tekapo and the Church of the Good Shepherd

BIBLIOGRAPHY

The Scots of New Zealand	G.L. Pearce	Dundee	1976
The Southern Runs	J.H. Beattie	TPS	1979
Early South Canterbury Runs	Robert Pinney	Reed	1971
Early Northern Otago Runs	Robert Pinney	Collins	1981
Station Country I, II & III	Philip Holden	Hodder Moa Beckett	1993, 1995, 1997
NZ Agriculture – A Story of the Past 150 Years		NZ Rural Press	1990
A Southern Gentry	Stevan Eldred-Grigg		
MacKenzie of the MacKenzie Country Story of the Famous Sheep-Lifter	Herries Beattie	Otago Daily Times	1946
Early Runholding in Otago	Herries Beattie	Otago Daily Times	1947
On The Run	Vicki McRae	Crown Kerr Printing	1999
Stockman Country	B.Foster & V.Wright	Listener	1993
The Wakatipians	Alfred H. Duncan	John McIndoe	1888, 1964, 1969
Fall Muster	Philip Holden	Hodder & Saughton	1991
Glenary	Peter M. ChandlerCraigs		
Eight Daughters, Three Sons	Barbra Harper	Reed	
Historic Sheep Stations of New Zealand	Colin Wheeler	Beckett	1989
Station Days in Maoriland	George Meek	Omarau Mail Coy Ltd	1952
The Sparkling Waters of Whakatipu	Florence MacKenzie	Reed	1947
History of Northern Southland	G.A. Hamilton		1952
Early Canterbury Runs	L.G.D. Ackland	Whitcoulls	1930
Golden Days of Lake Country	F.W.G. Miller	Whitcoulls	1949
High Endeavour	William Vance	Reed	1965
Lion of Scotland	Neil Robinson	Birlinn	1952, 1999
The Settler Church	Peter Matheson		
Notes and memoirs (Mount Linton)	Douglas Pick		
Letter from Catherine Ann Cameron	(Ben Ohau)		1859-1860
Notes on Araparwanui	Mrs McKinnon		

Coll, on the highest hill, Cruachan, at home on Skye, with the Cuillin range in the background.

EILIDH MACPHERSON

Eilidh MacPherson is a farmers' daughter from the Isle of Skye. After graduating in Agriculture from Edinburgh University, Eilidh headed to Australia and New Zealand for a year and a half. She drenched 18 000 sheep, worked on a Merino Stud and drove a 30' cut combine harvester in Australia, before moving on to work in the shearing sheds in New Zealand.

Following a stint shepherding in the Scottish Borders she took up the handpiece and worked as a professional sheep shearer for several years, employing New Zealanders on Skye, then heading to the Antipodes for the winter.

Eilidh went on to manage a Scottish Lamb Group, work for Scottish Quality Beef and Lamb and then operate as an independent livestock agent on the West Coast before taking off to New Zealand again in 1999.

Taking part of NZ home by setting up and running Isle of Skye Shears led to reporting on the shearing competitions across the country and being 'paid per word rather than per sheep, without even getting a sweat up,' – a much easier option than shearing!

Since then Eilidh has written full time for two and half years for the New Zealand Farmer Magazine and has freelanced for: New Zealand Shearing Magazine, Otago Southland Farmer, High Country Herald, Southland Times, Straight Furrow, Oban Times, West Highland Free Press, Scotsman and Scottish Farmer.

On her return to Scotland she established her own title – farmingscotland.com magazine – a free monthly national paper available in livestock markets, farm shops, tractor dealers and Department Offices across the county. The magazine runs a Young Farmer of the Year Competition – another Kiwi concept.

From Thistle to Fern has enabled Eilidh to merge her interest in photography with her passion for sheep and the High Country of New Zealand.

Growing up on a hill sheep and beef farm in the Highlands, Eilidh has always been intrigued by the ruined villages, the Highland Clearances and the resulting diaspora. Meeting and working with the station owners and shepherds, researching and writing the book gave her an amazing insight into life in the High Country, past and present.

Eilidh is a Director of the Highland Livestock Heritage Society, which aims to erect a life size bronze sculpture of a Highland bull and drover at the entrance to the new livestock market in Dingwall. The mart will house archives regarding the economic and social history of the Scottish livestock industry and its people.